ROD AND LINE

ROD AND
❧ LINE ❧

ARTHUR RANSOME

Oxford New York
OXFORD UNIVERSITY PRESS

Oxford University Press, Walton Street, Oxford OX2 6DP

London Glasgow New York Toronto
Delhi Bombay Calcutta Madras Karachi
Kuala Lumpur Singapore Hong Kong Tokyo
Nairobi Dar es Salaam Cape Town
Melbourne Auckland

and associates in
Beirut Berlin Ibadan Mexico City Nicosia

First collected and published by Jonathan Cape 1929
First issued as an Oxford University Press paperback 1980
Reprinted 1982

British Library Cataloguing in Publication Data

Ransome, Arthur
Rod and Line. - (Oxford paperbacks).
1. Fishing
I. Title   II. Series
799.1' 1' 08   SH439   79–41654
ISBN 0–19–281278–5

Printed in Great Britain by
Cox & Wyman Ltd
Reading, Berks

To
the Most Long-Suffering of Fishermen's
Wives

Note

The fifty papers here collected under the general heading of ROD AND LINE have appeared during the last few years in the *Manchester Guardian*, to the Editor of which I am indebted for his kind permission to reprint them.

A.R.

Contents

Contents

On Tackle-shops

The pleasures of fishing are chiefly to be found in rivers, lakes and tackle-shops and, of the three, the last are the least affected by the weather. The sight of rods in a window brings a fisherman to a full stop as surely as the sight of a bridge. In such weather as we have been having, when fishing is all but impossible, a fishing-tackle-shop has a magnetic power that can be felt over a considerable area. We are conscious, for example, of a shop in the City Road when we are at the further end of Deansgate and of a shop in Moult Street while we are dodging trams at the corner of Albert Square. These are the shops we know. But it is the same in strange towns. There too, there seems to be a mistaken idea that the centre of the town is some Town Hall, or Public Library, or Square decorated with political gods in stone or bronze, when, if the truth were known, the whole town is grouped about some little shop where a man will find, in the window, boots and pike tackle, Mayflies and flat-irons, and behind the counter a fisherman like himself. Let him go in there and he is in a strange town no longer. There, at least, he has the passwords and is allowed to taste the brotherhood of man. In these shops there is nothing but good will, except towards polluters of rivers. Again and again I have gone into a tackle shop in a strange town lonely and dispirited and come out blithe as a blackbird on his own lawn. Of course there are shops in which fishing-tackle is no more than grocery, stuff to be sold, but these are not shops kept by fishermen and they do not last long. In the right shops is always the atmosphere of a good fishing day. Inside those shops all is confidence. All men are Selwyn Marryats and all fish are not fools, but not so clever that we shall not catch

1

them. A rosy glow enhances our memories, from which, somehow, our bad days are expunged. It is a pleasure to see other
men buying fishing-tackle, a pleasure to feel that their confidence is also yours, a pleasure to cast forward with them in
imagination to the riverside. It is a pleasure to see the tackle,
some of it confirming your own choice in the past, some of it
promising happy extravagance in the future. It would be gross
ingratitude not to acknowledge the warmth of feeling that is
given by the delightful sight of an old lady selling pennyworths
of maggots to small boys. The sort of shop that can be counted
on is the shop where the small boy who asks for a penny hook
is given a twopenny one with a handful of maggots thrown in.
In such a shop I do not mind being sometimes overcharged.
Such a shop is kept only by a fisherman. That is the secret. No
one cares a hang whether his grocer takes sugar in his tea or
whether he takes tea at all. But the pleasure of a visit to a
tackle-shop depends a great deal upon the knowledge that at
the week-end the tackle-dealer will be fishing like his customer.
All the great tackle-dealers were good fishermen. I think of
J. W. Martin, the 'Trent Otter'; of poor Walbran, who was
drowned while grayling fishing (well I remember visits to his
shop as a small boy, with my father); and of the friend so many
Manchester fishermen have lost in the late Mr John Pendrigh.

It is as mistaken to think that we go to tackle-shops only
because we need tackle as to think that we go fishing only
because we want to eat fish. Most fishermen dislike eating fish
and do their best not to buy tackle. It is just because the tackle-
dealer is a fisherman himself that he can be so extraordinarily
tolerant of his customers. For there are two distinct kinds of
visits to tackle-shops, the visit to buy tackle and the visit which
may be described as Platonic when, being for some reason
unable to fish, we look for an excuse to go in and waste a tackle-
dealer's time. Of this the tackle-dealer is well aware. He knows,
at once, as one of us comes through the door what kind of visit
is intended. The man who looks at his watch, raps out his order

in accurate detail, half a dozen each of Brunton's Fancy and
Little Marryat with two casts tapered to 4x, is going grayling
fishing and wants from the dealer nothing but efficiency. That
other, a little shy, whose eyes wander from the rods in their
khaki cases to the glass-fronted cupboard of reels, from the
artificial minnows to the flies, from them to the labelled boxes
on the shelves, who modestly suggests that another customer
shall be served before himself (to give him an excuse for staying
longer in the shop) is in a different category. The one has come
because he is going fishing. The other is there because, alas, he
is not. The one wants tackle, the other a course of mental
treatment. Such is the noble nature of tackle-dealers that in
most cases he gets it.

In this matter the really good tackle-dealer can put doctors
and even solicitors to shame. He could give lessons to diplomatists. None, so well as he, knows how to suffer fools. Everyman,
while at his tackle-dealer's, is made to feel that he is something
of a fisher, that his praise of this or that is praise worth having,
that he is, indeed, the very man the tackle-dealer is glad to talk
fishing with. And if Everyman does, at his tackle-dealer's,
spend rather more than the small amount he had decided to
stand himself when he came in, why he comes out with a moral
tonic that is worth the money many times over, and he has the
tackle too. It is the moderation of the tackle-dealer that is so
admirable, for he has his visitor at his mercy. Of course, he
must not be tempted too far. The visitor, if he is wise, will keep
his talk to the safe subjects. It is not safe to mention reels and,
if the conversation approaches the point at which rods begin
to come out of their cases, he had better remember an appoint-
ment; or, if he really wants to play with fire, announce firmly
that he does not mean that day to buy a rod. The tackle-dealer
will tell him that he need not think of buying one, but will let
him handle the magic wands just the same. Magic they are and
the dealer knows it and so should Everyman, who must in this
crisis continually count over in his mind the long row of rods

he has already. A rod bought on one of these Platonic visits to a tackle-shop is never the pleasure that a rod is which has been bought, so to speak, on purpose. The Platonic visit should retain its character to the end. There is no harm in paying for it by the purchase of a few flies (which will always 'come in some time'), or some gut or a packet of hooks. But major purchases introduce an element that may destroy the otherwise salutary effect of the visit. A packet of flies can be hidden in the pocket and from the conscience, but to have to carry through the streets a brand-new rod as a proof that you have needed comfort on account of an inability to go fishing is a searing experience, not to be easily forgotten. This is, of course, well known to the superlative tackle-dealer, who will even put a rod away rather than take advantage of a customer's weakness (and we are often very weak) to inflict upon him a humiliation difficult to forgive. Bad tackle-dealers, who are not fishermen, take their chance and lose their customers. No man likes to revisit the scene of a public loss of his self-control.

The First Day at the River

The pleasure of the first day at the river begins some months before it. It is in its beginning a little quiet, rippling pleasure, like a stream near its source, made up of all kinds of imaginings too remote to be very disturbing. It swells as time goes on. Tributaries join it, such as the pleasure on some cold winter's day of tying a few flies ready for the season, visits to fishing-tackle shops, a letter from a friend showing that he has not forgotten that you and he decided last year that you would open this season together, occasional inspections of tackle, oilings of reels, small varnishings, and other excuses for taking your fly-rod from its case. A trout scale clinging to the cork handle since last year has a quite notable effect when you discover it unexpectedly. The little, almost secret stream of pleasure swells gradually as the day draws near, and if the day is long postponed the effect is like that of damming up a river. A day or two before you do at last get to the water you are likely to answer absent-mindedly if people question you on less important matters and to talk too long if they happen to mention the one subject which is now in almost complete possession of you. On the eve of the day you plan to go to bed early in order to be able to catch the morning train without loss of sleep, but do, as a matter of fact, go to bed later than usual. In spite of all your long expectation there is so much to be thought of at the last minute, so many things that must not be forgotten, besides a sort of exaltation that would not let you sleep even if you were to go upstairs to bed. The proper thing to do on the eve of your first day at the rivers is to lose a game of chess. You will have no chance of winning it unless your opponent is a fisherman and unless he, too, is visiting the river for the first time next day. But you can play and lose with a good heart and the utmost equanimity, your mind fluttering to and fro between the winding river that you have not seen since last year, and the chess-board which, with its rectangular squares, its mathematical precision, is the greatest possible contrast to it.

Lord Grey, in an incomparable paragraph, has described going to the railway station to go fishing thirty years ago. He said that the best way to get the utmost relish out of that, when living in London, was to walk over Westminster Bridge, and to neglect the hansom cabs, in some way different from all others, that were to be found at certain places by those who looked for them in the early morning. The best way today is to get there as quickly as possible, for, with all your preparations, you will be running it fine for the train. Also a scurry through the town at the last minute is the best prelude for the leisure of the riverside. It is like the pepper with Keats put in his mouth the better to enjoy the coolness of claret. It is good, however, if, on the way to the station, you get a glimpse of trees, in bud or young leaf. The chalk stream season opens late enough for that, and even with our earlier northern opening trees in Manchester contrive to give us some foretaste of the spring. The train journey, no matter how well you know it, will take longer than you expect. But, after you get out of the train, the further journey to the riverside is short, no matter how long you take about it. You are already there and ashamed of your previous hurry. You prolong these last moments instead of trying to shorten them. But you discover a curious indifference as to what you are to have for supper and accept without question the suggestions of the inn or lodging keeper.

I never take out my fly-rod and put it together at the riverside for the first time in the season without an uncanny fear that I have forgotten what little I have ever learnt. I would always rather make my first cast in private. Last Saturday, visiting one of the smaller Hampshire chalk streams for the first time since getting back to England, I did not begin fishing until I had seen my companion, about a field away, rise and lose a fish. His season, at least, had begun well. It would be a rare bad omen to hook and catch the first fish you rise. The three miracles should come singly. The first is that your line does, after all, shoot out and that your fly does, after all, drop splashless on the water. The second is that a fish rises to your fly. If you were not to miss it you would be cramming the second and third miracles into one, for the third and properly separate miracle is that when you rise a trout again you find with a surprise new each year that you have hooked it. With any luck that first fish will be undersized, and you will put yourself on good terms with the stream by putting it back, not throwing it, but dropping it gently in the quiet water at the edge and seeing it suddenly realize that it is free. After that you are fishing in earnest, and there is little to distinguish your first day of the season from any other day's fishing. Although, perhaps, in each year you get a particular satisfaction from the first of many small experiences, that will become habitual before the season is over. There is a little extra delight in the first flash of a moving fish that you notice under water, the first sight of a feeding fish approaching your fly before he breaks the surface, the first detection from, for example, the behaviour of bubbles, that there is in some unlikely place a bit of slow-moving water which should hold a good fish, and the first triumph when that good fish, so detected, proves you right by taking a firm hold of your fly when you drop it carefully just within reach of him. You are rather like a child going through its whole vocabulary and delighted by the successful remembrance of each word.

The first day of the season should not end with an empty basket. It is not likely to, for the trout are as unaccustomed to the angler as he to them. But there is no need that it should end with a full one. It would be out of nature and disheartening to make one's best basket on the opening day. No, it should be a day like last Saturday, ending for the two of us with nothing to quarrel about, four brace and three and a half, the best fish being with the man who had caught the lesser number, and the two baskets emptied in the evening making a handsome sight upon a decent dish. And, even if everything has gone just as it should, perhaps the greatest satisfaction of the first day of the season is the knowledge in the evening that the whole of the rest of the season is to come.

North-Country Fishing Ninety Years Ago

In a second-hand bookshop I found a little brown book, dedicated to Christopher North, 'clarissimo viro, Piscatori, poetae, critico; Calamo, tam piscatorio quam scriptorio, Apprime perito, Fuste (Hibernicè, *shillelah*) formidabili, Scipione (Anglicè, *crutch*) tremendo,' by Stephen Oliver the Younger, published in 1834. In the book was an old envelope with a postmark of 28 April 1841 addressed to the Rev J. C. Atkinson, then staying at Fawley Court, Ross, Herefordshire, and no doubt fishing in the Wye. Was this the Rev J. C. Atkinson who wrote of Jack of Danby Dale and Goathland and was a noted angler in his day? On the back of the envelope in pencil are scribbled the dressings of five flies, three for the Conway and two for the Dee. For the envelope alone I would have bought the book. But the book itself is a spirited performance and particularly interesting to those whose fishing is north of Trent and south of Tweed. It is called *Recollections of Fly-fishing*, but is very free with its title, including long quotations from Juliana Berners, dialogues partly in the manner of Walton and partly (by imitation) complimentary to the *Noctes Ambrosianae*, and a sketch of a fishing tour through the northwest counties.

Stephen Oliver was an enthusiast and a good man, for, as he tells us, 'fishing never engaged the attention of a bad.' He reminds us that Paley was painted with his fishing-rod, that Nelson continued to fish after he had lost an arm, and, as a proof that fishing conduces to longevity, cites the case of Mr Henry Jenkins, who lived to the age of 169 'and boasted, when giving evidence in a court of justice to a fact of 120 years' date, that he could dub a fly as well as any man in Yorkshire.' His

9

passion for Wordsworth does not impair his delight in rude cheerful verse into which his dialogues often break. He quotes the song of a Coquet angler on the subject of the Red Hackle:

> The black-flee is guid when its airly;
>   The may-flee is deadly in Spring;
> The midge-flee may do in fair weather,
>   For foul sawmon, roe is the king;
> But let it be late or be airly,
>   The water be drumly or sma',
> Still up wi' the bonny red heckle,
>   The heckle that tackled them a'.

He has a scornful word for coarse fishing, and lets one of his characters exclaim that if he had the bad fortune to live in London he would put aside his rods and never fish again. Southern rivers are too smooth for him. He is for a background of fells, not water-meadows, and for a stream with a song to it, not silent as an eel. His dialogues end with a cheerful stave:

> Anglers all, good night, good night!
>   Sweet be your sleep and sound;
> Be early up with the morning light,
>   Ere the dew hath left the ground.
>   (All retire, singing.)

When the persons of his 'Piscatorial Nights' have thus gone vociferously to bed, he settles down to tell his reader how to make an 'angling tour among the hills' and to cast a fly in place after place well loved by anglers of today. The fisherman is 'to make his way to York as he most conveniently can, either by the mail, post-coach, or in his own carriage.' From York he is to send to Kendal his travelling trunk, 'containing merely a change of shirts and Wordsworth's poems, excepting the volume which he will constantly carry in his pocket.' Then with rod and creel slung across his back he is to set out on foot, carrying in his creel an extra shirt and a pair of stockings 'packed in oilskin', to take a grayling in the Ure at Masham. Then he is to make his way to Sedbergh by Askrigg, fishing down Garsdale on the way. Then he is advised to fish down the Lune by Middleton and Underley to Kirkby Lonsdale, but not to neglect the higher reaches either, and only when he has sufficiently exercised his skill in this neighbourhood to walk over to Kendal, get clean linen from his trunk, change one volume of Wordsworth for another, and send the trunk on to await him at Keswick. In those days, seemingly, anglers did not bother much about getting permissions to fish, but even today a wandering fisherman could get a day or two on much of this water by buying tickets locally.

Stephen Oliver was a fly-fisher but no purist. He tells his reader not to take his place in the coach for Shap before 'providing himself with a stock of brandling worms and gentles' from the tanyards in Kendal. With these as a stand-by as well as his flies he may fish the Lowther down to Askham and is told he may sleep at Pooley Bridge, and spend a day on Ullswater. If by good fortune a thunderstorm catches him on the lake, 'let him directly lay in his oars, that nothing may divert his mind from the contemplation of the scene.' That sentence alone would date the book. Should the Eamont be rather high, the fishermen may expect to get a score of fish between ten and twelve ounces each in a couple of hours. He would be a happy man if he did as much today. He may then come to Keswick, but will find Derwentwater over-fished and not worthy of an angler's attention. Derwentwater in those days was infested by scoundrels who fished with otter-boards and by a poet for whom Mr Oliver evidently did not feel the respect he felt for Wordsworth. Sitting one evening in a friend's garden at Keswick, 'he heard a strange discordant noise at the foot of the lake, which he mistook for the evening tattoo of a bittern,' till he was informed that it proceeded from Mr Southey, who was exercising his voice the the good of his health. Bassenthwaite perch were as poor as they are today, but the Derwent, after passing through Bassenthwaite Lake, 'contains large trouts weighing from two to five pounds.' From

11

Keswick, after another change of shirts and poetry, the trunk
is to be sent to Ambleside, while the angler is to visit Butter-
mere and fish the Cocker down to Cockermouth. He is warned
that salmon fishing in the Derwent 'is but a dull recreation
after all,' and he does not wonder when Mr Oliver goes on to
tell him that the roe of salmon poached in the Derwent is sold
all over the North and used as a bait in the Annan, the Tweed,
the Wharfe, and Driffield Beck. He is then told to fish by
Ravenglass and in the Duddon, to come to Coniston by
Broughton, to fish Esthwaite (better than its bigger neighbours)
and so to the Ferry and Bowness. He may catch a pike in the
lake, have a look at the Langdales, and spend a day fishing the
Brathay. Then 'let the angler prepare for his return homeward,
but not until he has seen Wordsworth.' After he has seen
Wordsworth, he may take his seat on the Kendal coach and so
to Settle, York, and south to the haunts of the unblest.

Fishing in Books and Fishing in Fact

A succession of bad days and a library of fishing books have led me to the conclusion that there are two quite different kinds of angling and that the relation between the two is like that between Arcadia and normal country life. Fishing in print takes place in a golden age. If the sun shines there it shines not too brightly. A storm is deprived of all its wetting power. The wind, tamed and orderly, does not use casting lines for the making of fishermen's puzzles, but, if you are casting against it, separates like the Red Sea before the Israelites to let your flies slip through in Indian file and gossamer procession, and, if you cast with it, holds them suspended at any length you wish until you drop them, lighter than thistledown, to be engulfed upon the instant by three-pounders that follow you about to play their part in the happy pastoral scene. In books, a rise is a rise, a gold, spotted, heraldic fish flashes head and tail in the air or takes your fly with quiet decorum, you tighten with a turn of the wrist, play him down-stream, lead him down the central aisle through a congregation of other trout so intent upon a sermon, or the next paragraph of the book, that they notice him as little as well-behaved parishioners notice the noisy urchin being led out by the churchwarden. They must not notice him, for in the next paragraph it is their turn to take the fly and find their way in a manner as orderly as a minuet to the safe haven of your basket. In books the fish and the weather know their parts. They are word perfect, as the actors say. In books, so are you.

In books you observe, while you are setting up your rod, a flotilla of flies, sailing down-stream like little goosewinged schooners. You catch one, plucking it from the stream as you

13

would pluck a flower. In books there is no difficulty about that. You look at the fly and call it by its name. Then, in older books, you find in your dubbing bag a hare's ear, some hackles from a gamecock, some wool, some feathers from the starling's breast, and, in a single sentence, you make a fly, a little smaller than the original but otherwise exactly like it. In modern books, you open an aluminium box and find there, made by Cummins, or Hardy, or Farlow, the very fly you need. You put it on. Four simple words of one syllable each, so unlike the real life business of finding the eye with the gut, making one knot and then another, pulling two out in the process of making fast and finally breaking the gut in testing your handiwork by the gentlest tug. Then, of course, your gut straightens itself by magic and at the first cast you see the fly alight over the large trout that, quite undisturbed by your flycatching, is rising now and again, as if to remind you that he is waiting upon your convenience in putting your tackle together. Everything goes right and if you miss a rise you will be given another chance and have him. You lunch on the bank when the rise is over and contemplate your beauties, fairer than any picture, as decorations in your airy sylvan parlour. You do not hang your flies in hawthorn bushes, or, if you do, the incident is made delightful by your finding there the complete, undamaged cast of some less fortunate fisherman. There are no wasps, or if there are they busy themselves in driving away a bull who might otherwise have annoyed you. There are no little boys. There are no other anglers until, just as you are taking your rod to pieces to go home, one who has had a day's fishing not in books, an ordinary day's fishing, stops beside you, and before he has seen into your crammed basket, tells you that the river is out of order and that it is little wonder that the fish are taking nothing.

Writers of angling books must be men of weak memories upon whose callous brains only the most memorable events make sharp impression. They write at Christmas time, or between Christmas and the opening of the season, if they be trout fishermen, or in the months of April and May if they be fishermen for pike or roach. Only the most memorable moments of the past season are in their minds, and they sweeten their recollections with their hopes of the season that is to come. Opportunity lacks to test their good resolves. They are determined to have no bad habits by the waterside and so they have none in their studies. If the weather be unpropitious, it is all the more promising for the time of which they think, and if it be a perfect day as they look up from their desks, they add its perfection to the fishing that they are putting upon paper.

Of fishing in fact there is hardly need to write. There is not a fly on the river. If there is, you cannot catch it. If you catch it you have nothing like it in your expensive collection. You miss rise after rise. You try smaller flies, get more rises and miss them too. You begin to put more force into your strike and presently break a hook in the mouth of a good fish, miss the next four rises from being too tender and lose your fly over the fifth. You notice a good fish under a big smooth stone in the opposite side of the river. Remembering the books, you cast so as to drop your fly on the stone, from which it is to fall, as an insect might and be engulfed by the monster. That smooth stone, even as you cast, cracks imperceptibly, receives your fly into the crack and holds it fast. You have to wade across to release it and as you wade disturb a much larger fish in a much easier place. The water gurgles in over your wading stockings. You have to pull for a break and lose the last specimen you have of the fly that has been getting all the rises. At last you hook a fish decidedly under size, so badly that you have to kill him, at which moment the water bailiff strolls up and you have to explain to him. He pretends to believe you and asks to see the rest of your catch. He then tells you that Mr X a little further down has been having a very good day, and suggests that you should put on the fly that you have just lost. Finally after fishing till dusk, you set off home. On the way, you take a cast, just for luck, in a place where you missed a good one, and get caught up in a tree behind you. You break your cast, strain the middle joint of your rod in taking it to pieces, find that you left the stoppers where you put your rod up, it being now too dark to look for them, tell yourself that after all stoppers do not matter, and in taking off your waders learn that they have been torn by a bramble. In all this I have said nothing about the weather. Suffice it that at starting out you have told your wife that it is too good a fishing day to miss.

Familiar Rivers

Familiar things caught my eyes as I dropped into the valley, from which the distant mountains have different profiles from those to which I am now accustomed. It was very like coming home, after long absence. The blackthorn in the hedge by the road that runs close by the river (and so far has not been tarred, nor ever will be, let us hope), was glittering with promise. The warmth had held, a steady, comfortable warmth, so that it would be possible to fish with coat unbuttoned. No man likes fishing in a closed waterproof coat, even when it is necessary. The night's drizzle was over. It was as if it had not been, like the early morning charwoman who does her good work and disappears. There were clouds in the sky, chasing the sun but never quite catching him. And, as I put my rod up, on the bank from which, in short knickerbockers, I used to paddle my feet in the water, the steady murmur of the stream was not enough to drown a definite 'plop' as a quarter-pounder turned a somersault out of the water and into it again. Much of the river is shrouded by trees and opening buds are well adapted to catch flies, but today the twigs were not yet so well covered as to make disentangling any serious test of character. The water was cool but not cold. There was, as I had hoped, just enough of it in the river. This river, except when in spate, is one abnormally clear in which the trout, though not large, have the reputation of being shy risers. They certainly would not rise to the wet fly today except in those few places where the current markedly stirs the surface to the angler's advantage. The only way to catch them was with the floating fly. Oddly, for I put it on with a complete lack of that faith which is usually necessary, the fly that tricked them best was one of Mr Dunne's duns. I saw no natural fly on the water like it, but when trial of several others had failed I put on Mr Dunne's dun, less in hopes of fish than for my own sake, because it was easy to see as it came sliding down the smooths and dancing over the ripples, and from the moment this pale fairy showed on the stream, fish began to come to net or hand (mostly to hand–I had to return over a score), and every now and then one was put in the basket. There was nothing of any size, but they were good enough fish for the river. The whole point of Mr J. W. Dunne's invention is the translucent effect of his flies' bodies, and I remembered Mr Nelson saying that the body of a fly is what matters. The body is what the trout wants. He does not care about the wings. However this might be, I observed with gratitude that I was enjoying myself prodigiously.

It occurred to me to wonder how much of that enjoyment was due to those duns and how much was independent of the catching of fish, but due to the pleasure of fishing, nearly forty years after, the first river I knew in childhood, in one of the tributary becks of which I caught my first trout with a bent pin and a hazel stick. Every length of the river had its memory for me. The first stretch led me up to the little wooden footbridge. The little bridge is sadly broken down, but the raised causeway of stones beside the path leading to it still stands and no doubt, in time of spate, delights other children as once it delighted me, a firm footway through the swirling brown waters. The next stretch is from the wooden bridge to the old bobbin mill, now in ruin, which I remember as a busy place with a smell of fresh wood shavings. There is a long deep dub below the bobbin mill, where my father over thirty years ago caught a fine mort, when the screeching of the old-fashioned reel could be heard (I can hear it yet) at the mill, while the fisherman was invisible round the bend below. I looked for my boyhood's friend, the dipper, under the stone bridge, and he was there. The same peewits were calling that were calling so long ago and, when at last I climbed up to the road to tramp down the valley again in the dusk, an owl, the very one I used to hear from the farm at night after going to bed (How they curtail our days in childhood!), hooted in the woods where in those days we knew there were badgers. I daresay there are badgers there yet.

Now all this was in some sort a proof that I too was the same, a proof to me at least. Today time was not. I have fished plenty of rivers in which there are better fish, but no other river ever gives me that same surprising, delightful feeling that the hands of the clock have in very fact been set back. I have always known why fishermen, who know a river well, are absent-minded in towns. I know today how it is that men who never leave the river they knew as children measure old age exclusively by its physical effects. Wise doctors with patients who seek their lost youth should countersign my lay prescription and tell them to cross the world if necessary to fish their first river.

In Memoriam: William Nelson

Few who fish the length of the Eden between Wild Boar Fell and Armathwaite will come to their river this year (1926) without a feeling that Eden will never be the same again. The river has lost a great fisherman who will be remembered long after all of us have laid rod and creel away for the last time. William Nelson was a schoolmaster and a golfer. I knew him as neither, though I believe he drove a straight ball and, teaching the deaf and dumb, did noble work in his profession. But it was fishing that he cared for most and he knew the Eden as few men knew it. He had learnt to fish there as a boy (from good masters, though it is hard to think of anyone teaching him who taught so many). Every boulder in the river, each glide and stickle, had a memory for him. He would walk along its banks and from the experience of fifty years would tell his companion (for he was as pleased to fill other men's baskets as his own), 'You should have one there,' or 'There is usually a fish at this time on the far edge of that bit of stream,' or 'Just above the rock and you have him.' He exulted in his friends' catches for his friends' sake and also because they showed his beloved river in a good light. And what catches he had made there himself . . . on that day, for example, when someone had put him on his mettle by saying that the Eden needed re-stocking. Re-stocking! He would show them. And he did.

He was a master of all the methods of fishing used on the Eden, though he liked some better than others. He did not care much for bustard fishing or night-fishing generally, though I have some notes on the best flies for that purpose which he gave me for use on that river when the season for this fishing comes round. He preferred fly-fishing to any other and, though he was not an exceptional caster, could catch fish when fine casters could not. He was a great hand at creeper-fishing, for which he had invented some ingenious artificial insects, and few could beat him in the use of the minnow, when the water was 'copper-coloured', after a flood. For this last purpose he used a Malloch reel and was proud that he had worn one out and prouder still that a friend of his had made it as good as new for him. He used with this reel a short greenheart spinning rod, not more than seven or eight feet in length. With this he had the prettiest knack of dropping his minnow splashless where he wished. He used natural minnows, salted and dried, on flights made by himself. He used to say that Windermere minnows had special efficacy for Eden trout. One day last summer, when there was nothing to be done with fly, I watched him giving a lesson in the use of the minnow to a young golfer who was newly taken to fishing. That friend of his who had mended his reel for him was there also, and we sat a little way back on the bank in the sunshine and observed master and pupil. The water was that rapid glide under the Castle Rock at Appleby, the very place where Mr Nelson had himself learnt to fish in boyhood. Two or three times he tossed his minnow across the stream, and then handed the rod to his pupil, pointing out the little flick of the forward swing, the need to avoid force, the way to bring the hands conveniently to turn the reel as the bait reached the water. The pupil did not do so badly. Then Mr Nelson, taking the rod again, to give a final example, moved a pace or two down-stream, opposite the end of the trees, where the swift glide passes over a boulder or two and widens into a broad smooth stream, good for grayling in winter. 'Now if there were a fish here,' he said, 'and you were to drop your minnow just there, under the far bank' (casting as he spoke) 'you might have him.' There was a sudden quiver of the rod and a moment or two later a fine fat trout of three-quarters of a pound was played across to the shelving gravel. It might have been a picture from the *Compleat Angler*, with Mr

Nelson as Piscator and his young golfing friend taking Venator's part.

He was never happier than when showing other people the
secrets of his river and many looked upon him with the
reverence with which he himself looked back to his own
masters. Many who had never seen him handling a rod or
making up a cast or a minnow tackle (his minnow tackles were
better than any that money can buy) or heard his eager vivid
talk by the riverside when the rise was off, or over his fireside
when there was no fishing to take him from it, think of him as
if they knew him from having read his book. 'Fishing in Eden'
will be read by fishermen of Eden as long as the river runs
under the Castle Rock. It is one of the few modern fishing
books certain of its longevity, a book crammed with intimate
knowledge and as simple-hearted as the old fisherman, 'Bob',
whose remarks in the Westmorland dialect are scattered
through its pages. I have read that book a dozen times and
never without finding something in it new and valuable.

Mr Nelson had been asked to write a volume on the grayling,
a fish for whose presence in the Eden he felt a kind of responsibility since an uncle of his, forty years ago, had tipped the first
tub full of those fish into the river, during a spate, salving his
conscience with the half hope that they would be carried out
to sea. Mr Nelson was always ready to defend the grayling, had
a liking for him and knew him extremely well, but, with
characteristic modesty was unwilling to write a book on him
lest people should think he was trying to supersede Pritt's
classic. He had other writings on hand when he died and was
looking forward to retiring to Appleby with the opening of the
trout season there to write and to fish in the river that had been
his passion since boyhood. Last summer he was busy preparing
the cottage where he was to live. Close by the churchyard he
speaks of in his book, within sound of the river, he was to
spend the old age that was denied him. There were to be roses
in his garden. He was to watch them grow on the trellis he had

fixed on his cottage walls. There was a rod room, where he could keep his rods set up and walk out with them across the road and down to the riverside. Last autumn he was there for a day or two, caught a leash of grayling at his favourite place, and left his rod with reel and line upon it, ready for the next time.

The Benign Moment

The benign moment is difficult to define or explain, though
every fisherman knows it. It is like one of those sudden silences
in a general conversation when, in England, we say, 'An angel
passes' and in Russia, in the old days, they used to say, 'A
policeman is being born.' The day is not that day but another.
Everything feels and looks different. The fisherman casts not
in the mere hope of rising a fish but, knowing that he will rise
one, concerned only to hook it when it comes. He knows that
even the hooking of it is more likely than at other times.
Weather, river and fish seem suddenly to be on the angler's
side and prepared to do their best for him. This is not the
moment to be wasted in putting on a fresh cast. Hawthorn
trees seem to know this and, joining in the happy conspiracy,
skilfully evade the flies that in moments not benign they reach
out to clutch greedily behind the angler's back. Or is it that in
these moments, trout rise so near the fisherman that he is never
tempted to lengthen his line in dangerous places? But in other
moments all places are dangerous. Flies cling to moss, to
stones, to clothing, whirl themselves tightly round the rod or,
in an instant, turn a straight piece of fine gut into a cat's
cradle. When this last happens, wise fishermen take it as a
kindly indication that the moment is not benign and that their
flies may as well not be on the water. If they swear they do so
with such good temper and even gratitude that their words fall
like a caress. They do not pull off the cast to be disentangled
at home, but, there and then, sit down patiently at the riverside, observe with calm pleasure a wagtail or a dipper, enlarge
their souls to leisure, and, without hurry, reduce the cat's
cradle to order, stretch the cast anew and know that they have

lost no time, no good time, at all. And when this elaborate business is finished, if they do not arise suddenly with violence and stride with determination up-stream, they have a good chance of being rewarded in other coin beside that of moral satisfaction in which, already, they have been richly paid. Half a dozen sand-martins may be skimming the water, picking up from above their share of a hatch of flies that the trout will be attacking from below. More: trout may be rising in the very water which the angler left when he came ashore to do his disentangling. The fish that was put down by being offered the tangle of gut that it was not his business to unravel, may now be rising again and ready to take the fly that was in that tangle, now happily straightened out. Again and again it happens that the benign moment follows immediately upon a moment so far from benign that it has compelled the fisherman to give the river a rest.

So often, indeed, does this happen that I am sometimes tempted to think that the benign moment is a wholly subjective affair, that it is less a state of river than a state of mind and that when we are told to take a rest when we are fishing badly, we are really being told to create, artificially, a benign moment for ourselves. But, when actually fishing, I am quite sure that the benignity of the happy moment, when it comes, is not of my making, is not dependent upon me and is dependent on some subtle combination of circumstances not under my control. It is a meteorological, not a psychological phenomenon. And with that I am back again at the difficulty, not so much of defining it as of explaining it, of analysing it into its component parts. I sometimes fancy that it depends on some slight change in atmospheric pressure. This would explain why it seems not only to make the trout more willing to rise and to take flies well into the back of their mouths, but also to improve the fisherman. I fancy that if, in addition to all the tackle we already carry with us (we could not do it if we had as many fish to carry as our grandfathers), we had with us barographs of sensitive nature, registering changes of pressure so that we could observe them from hour to hour and even from minute to minute, we should find that the benign moments of which we were conscious would be marked in some way in the line traced by the barograph's recording needle. Those moments are not to be explained simply as coincident with a hatch of fly. In moments other than benign flies may sail down river in Armadas without the slightest effect on our baskets. And, in any case, how judge between cause and effect? A hatch of fly does usually seem to accompany a benign moment, but may not the flies, like the trout and the fisherman, be encouraged by the moment instead of being its cause. Then, too, on our swiftly varying rivers, it is possible that prolonged observation would show that the benign moments would be indicated in some way on a curve that should represent from minute to minute the rising and falling of the water. For example, a benign moment often occurs when the river first shows to the fish signs that it is going to rise. To the fish, I say, for they know all about it before the duller angler has drawn his deductions from the flotsam carried on the stream, the first dry leaves picked from its shores as the river, higher up, brimmed above the line at which they had been left. And when, after a freshet, the river clears, such moments are sometimes to be enjoyed. But here, we seem to be considering good conditions for angling in general rather than the conditions of those rare moments that sometimes make the difference between a blank day and one on which the returning angler sings or whistles in the dusk. The benign moment proper occurs, and is most noticeable when it does occur, in a day on which the conditions for fishing are, in general, poor.

Perhaps on account of our unsettled weather and uncertain streams, the benign moment may be considered as a phenomenon characteristic of north country fishing. On the equable chalk streams it occurs, but is, somehow, less important. On the prettiest chalk stream in England I have known a dull hour to be followed by this miraculous change, as if I had closed my eyes for a moment and opened them on a different day, as if a wand had been waved and a spell loosed by some invisible being in the water-meadows. In the south, however, the coming or not coming of the benign moment is not one of the chief interests in the day. Whereas, with us, the possibility of its coming is the thing that enables us to put up with much hardship and disappointment. In this weather, with the barometer jumping up and down like a grasshopper, with the river one foot in drought and one in flood, to one thing constant never, the hope of the benign moment sustains the fisherman through many barren hours and sometimes puts something in his basket at the end of them.

On Giving Advice to Beginners

Fortunately, in fishing, we are beginners all. Fishing is not like billiards, in which it is possible to attain a disgusting perfection. It is not like chess, in which a sharp line seems to be drawn between those who play badly enough to enjoy the game and those who play so well that they have lost all spirit of adventure and haggle over pawns like misers over pence. The older a fisherman grows the more conscious is he that he has much to learn and he lays aside his rod in the end as a man dies knowing that all his effort has left him but a bungler. The better a fisherman is, the more conscious is he of his imperfections and consequently the more shy of giving advice to others. He is also likely to have learnt that the chief pleasure of fishing is to be still beginning and, unselfishly, he will be very unwilling to steal from a beginner any of the delight of finding out for himself. Long as the road is, distant the happily unattainable goal, the fisherman who has relished each stage of his journey feels that he is cheating his friend if he shows him a short cut. He is more inclined to give too little advice than too much. The way of the beginner, of the man who is really beginning to be a beginner, is consequently hard. It must seem to him that he is among priests who are determined to keep the mysteries of their cult.

I fished a little while ago with a man, not in his first youth, who had wasted the flower of his life on business and golf and gardening and motoring and marriage, and had in this way postponed his initiation far too long. It was his second season. In his first season he had caught six trout. This season he had begun with hope and continued with determination, but he had caught no fish and was a little disheartened. His master had been much too good a fisherman. It is only young Know-all who tries to tell everything, but this man's initiator had been so good a fisherman that he had had hardly told his pupil anything at all. He had picked for him one of several second-hand rods, a small reel, a very fine tapered line and a handful of mixed flies and had put him by the river to catch trout. I watched him fishing, examined his weapons and decided that last season's six fish had been six several miracles. With that rather whippy rod, that fine line and that diminutive reel, his master could have done very well, but they were not the instruments to make casting easy for a middle-aged man who had not been apprenticed in boyhood. This unlucky beginner had been told to keep his fly dry and had been allowed to see his master doing this, but had not been told the secret of the oil-bottle, which his master is able to despise. Accordingly he approached the water (a little stream with no cover) whisked his rod backwards and forwards as fast and as hard as he possibly could, and then, with a colossal effort, lifting one foot from the ground and striking forward with all his strength, he tried to send his fly out. The result varied a good deal, because the final effort was made without any regard to the position of the whirling line above his head. If his cast had failed to entangle itself while it was being used in an attempt to whip the air into cream, it hit the water pretty hard. If it had time to straighten in doing this, which was seldom, the fly immediately dragged. If it fell in loops, the poor man withdrew it with an additional splash. Here was a case in which, speaking as one beginner to another, something had to be said.

He was so downcast that he even allowed me to cut about four yards of the taper off his line, so that the weight of the heavier part compelled the rod to do some work. It was a pleasure to see his surprise at the result. The hint that speed through the air was unnecessary cured his wild rod-wagging and the suggestion that he could always tell if he had made a decent cast by noticing if the pull of the line would take out another yard was enough to make him discover for himself the trick of shooting. The next suggestion was of a more questionable character. It was that it was just as well to learn to catch fish with a wet fly before attempting the more delicate though often easier task of catching them with a dry. Within five minutes of wetting his fly and abandoning his more violent forms of exertion he had a rise from the best fish any of us saw that day. The effect of this rise was curious. It paralysed the fisherman. Up came the trout, with a head as big as my fist. The rod bent. The fish was on. But the fisherman was like a man who had seen a vision. He stood open-mouthed for a great many seconds, then dropped his rod point and began winding that ridiculous little reel. The line, of course, fell slack and when, in response to urgent (and perhaps regrettable) cries, he lifted his rod point again the fish was gone. It had, however, turned him into a different man. Before, he had been asking whether it was not true that some men could never become fishermen. Now, he already regarded that fish as his and was prepared to fish for it for ever. He subsequently caught a little trout, but, remembering that monstrous head, rejected it as unworthy. There will be no stopping him now.

His discouragement had gone from him but his eagerness for knowledge was embarrassing to one who was determined not to tell him more than was good for him. Indeed he refused to be offended when told that stamping on the bank in casting was as bad as showing himself to the fish, though I fancy he did not believe it. He had a notion that he would fish better if he knew the names of his flies, and that evening I arranged them in his box for him, while he made a plan of the box on a bit of paper and wrote down their names in the right places. I warned him to copy Ulysses and to put wax in his ears when he heard men talk of flies, knowing, of course, that he would not do this but would add to his collection every time he passed a tackle-shop in town. We came to talk of knots. I had to show him the Turle and the easiest of all knots for fastening a line to a cast. He forgot them, I was glad to see, at once. I should otherwise have felt I was swindling him. Enough that he should see that it was possible to put on a fly so that it would not dangle or slip off, but too much if I had deprived him of the delight of learning for himself, by solitary experiment, how to do it. Not for anything would I lose my own happy memory of making sure of the blood-knot with a long suffering piece of string. That is the only honest way to treat beginners; to fend off from them, where you can, utter discouragement, but not, on any account, to tell them too much. They may think your reticence secretive. Twenty years later they will, if they have not forgotten it, understand that you were defending not your secrets but their pleasure.

Wading in Small Waters

It ought not to be necessary to point out to any fisherman that waders were invented to help people to catch fish and not to enable grown-up people to paddle without getting their feet wet. Paddling is a pleasure in itself, but it is best not to be too conscious of that pleasure while fishing. Unfortunately there are a number of men who seem to think that the wearing of waders almost compels them to paddle, and to paddle very deep. Those who have to fish a length of river with them must often be inclined to ask them whether they would not be happier at the seaside, where they could paddle in salt water without injury to their health, without wearing waders, without even encumbering themselves with a rod or a landing net, and without spoiling other folk's fishing. Not that the fisherman cannot enjoy his wading. There is a real pleasure in feeling the water pouring round your legs. The noise, the sensible motion of running water, and sometimes its strength, have an inspiriting effect upon the fishermen. A good salmon-fisherman had this in mind when he expressed his delight in 'sitting on the stream'. Fishing for grayling in winter, it is warmer in the river than out of it. All these things, and many like them, tempt us into the water. Nothing gives you such intimacy with the stream (barring tumbling in) as standing up against it. Also, there is no way of learning the bottom of a river so good as that of walking about on it. Even thoroughly bad wading may, on a subsequent day, turn to our advantage. Treading in a hole, we learn where, next day, to put our flies instead of our feet.

But, in so far as we go to the river to fish and not primarily to wade, all these things are temptations, particularly in small rivers, to sacrifice our fishing to our waders. There is only one safe rule. It is, never to wear wading trousers when stockings will do; never to wear stockings when you can fish as well without; and, if you must wear stockings, to wet them as little as possible. On a day when he does not have to cross the river a fisherman's pride should be to contrast the weight of his basket with the lowness of the high-water mark on his waders. In large waters deep wading cannot be helped, but, no matter where, waders should not be regarded as a bathing costume, dishonourable unless completely wetted. I am inclined to think that our ancestors were probably better waders than we are. They waded, when they needed to wade, in whatever they happened to be wearing. If a man knows that if he goes into the water his legs will be damp for the rest of the day, and that he himself is likely to acquire that 'stateliness in every joint' which other people than Sir Tophas know as rheumatism, he is unlikely to wade unless it is absolutely necessary. A new sumptuary law forbidding the use of waders by men under, say, your own age might be of great service to our craft. If a man has fished for many years without waders he is likely to know how very often with profit to himself he can keep out of the river.

No man can do justice to such rivers as the Eden or the Cumberland Derwent without wading, and sometimes, though not often, wading deep. There are lengths on most waters that can only be fished properly by a man standing in the river. But on some rivers wading is rightly forbidden altogether. On a small chalk stream, for example, a single man who wades muddies the water and spoils the fishing for a long way below him. Nor does wading help him to catch fish. It may give him the illusion that he is fishing in a larger stream than his own. It saves him, certainly, from the Red Indian work of crawling and creeping in the water-meadows, which is part of the fun of small chalk-stream fishing. But it saves him from these pleasures not to the advantage of his basket but at its expense. In such small, steady waters, where not even the most minute of cataracts divides one pool from another, frightened fish run far up-stream, spreading among the trout above the fisherman the news of the advent of a threatening kind of hippopotamus. On fast, much-broken streams, the wader does not do so much damage. Trout in such streams do not run so far when frightened, and the wader's clumsy hoofs do not raise so disgusting a cloud.

After an afternoon spent in watching three men fishing a small river, I come to the conclusion that the fishing books do not attribute sufficient importance to the technique of wading. They fill many pages with directions as to management of rod and line, prescribe a particular colour of dress, give just warnings against the casting of shadows, but fail altogether to impress upon their readers that unskilful wading may be worse than waving rod or than a wrong position with regard to the sun in the matter of making it difficult to catch fish. That afternoon the man who caught the most fish was by far the clumsiest with his rod but he was the cleverest with his legs. The others paddled. He never moved without remembering the fish. Before the others, as they moved up-stream, stretches that had been alive with rising trout fell dead. The other man seemed able to move until he was almost among the rising fish.

It is extremely difficult, in fishing quiet water, not to send a wave as you move that will drive all the trout from the shallows to spread their anxieties even among the fish in the stronger water at the neck. The only way to be sure of not sending these wireless but unmistakable messages is to have both feet on the bank. Where this man was fishing that was impossible, but I have never seen a man who seemed so well to realize, when he spotted a rising fish, that he had begun to fish for him long before he extended his line, at the moment he entered water that could carry a wave to the trout. It was clear that he knew that every step he was taking in that water was a part of his first cast. The result was to be seen in his basket. We are all careful over the actual making of our first cast to a fish, but, in our hurry to see our fly floating in the magic ring, it is very hard to remember that in the river, even more so than when stalking the fish from the bank, we have already begun to make that cast the moment we begin to move up after seeing the fish rise. Good wading can sometimes make up for indifferent casting, but the most perfect casting in the world will not restore confidence to a fish whose peace of mind has been disturbed by careless wading.

Beginners' Flies

In today's post-bag is the letter of a beginner who asks, with the large faith proper to his station, for lists of wet and dry flies to ensure that he shall enjoy 'reasonably good sport at any time during the season.' An older fisherman would know that unless we interpret the word 'reasonably' in a liberal manner, so as to admit as reasonably good sport a fair number of blank days, the drawing up of such a list is impossible. The beginner 'has endeavoured to master the contents of various books on the subject' and observes that the effort of making a selection from the hundreds of flies mentioned 'leaves him dizzy'. I don't wonder. Too many cooks spoil the broth, but, surely, the way to improve it is not to call in another cook. In asking me for a list, he is only asking to have his problem of choice made more difficult. Does he not realize that there is a reason for the differences between one man's list and another? Every fisherman makes his own. For a beginner to ask for a complete list of the necessary flies, that is to say for a list of all the flies that he will at one time or another come to think he needs, is to expect the gift of prophecy. Such a beginner is like a boy who sets out at the age of ten to buy all the clothes that he is likely to want in his lifetime. And I, asked to provide such a list, am in the position of the tailor, wondering whether he must cut for a tall man or a short, a fat or a scraggy one. The thing is not worth doing. Nor is it even desirable. Those wise doctors, over whose books our dizzy beginner has pored through the winter months, did not themselves begin with the long lists of flies they now recommend to him. The list of each man is the product of all the fishing he has done. The compilation of such lists, which swell rapidly as the fisherman learns the trout's catholicity of taste and then tend to shrink as he finds that it is not often necessary to pamper the fish by continually varying the bill of fare, is one of the pleasures of a trout-fisher's life. If I were to add my list to those which have already made my correspondent dizzy, I should only be increasing his dizziness and all to no purpose, because even if, in gratitude to me, he were to adopt my list and throw his books into the fire, he would still be without the list that, if he continues to fish, will some day be his own and not that of anyone else.

What then is the beginner to do? He is to fall in love with one fly after another. That is the secret of these long lists of flies. A man has a good day with Greenwell's Glory. He fishes it again and has another. Subsequent bad days are ascribed to the dourness of the fish until, one evening, he finds himself fishing vainly with a friend who is pulling them out on a Red Spinner. He borrows one and for a few days Red Spinner is the only fly. He then jilts Red Spinner and takes up with Wickham or Ginger Quill. Then there comes a day when he is in difficulties and he tries through the whole gamut of his old loves. And as the years go on the list of his loves lengthens and, when he comes to make a selection, each fly is remembered by him for the good days he had with it and he feels it unfair to leave it out. So, with ordinary fickle men. Even they, if they keep records, find on looking back that they can almost label their years by the names of the flies with which in those years they caught most fish. There are, however, a few constant heroes who never change their fly, and they, oddly enough, usually do pretty well. I know one man who is faithful to a Ginger Quill and another who on all waters and under all conditions fishes a Hirst's Fancy and always takes his share of trout. There are quite a number of men who are content with a March Brown. And some of the best fishermen who have ever lived have not needed more than half a dozen flies. Let the beginner, when he visits a tackle-shop, keep these facts sternly before him. In choosing his first dry flies, let him choose a very few flies of general usefulness, that is to say flies that resemble vaguely many insects and resemble none so closely that trout will refuse them when that insect is out of season.

In wet fly-fishing, the choice of a few flies is easier still. Long tradition, the accumulated experience of generations of fishermen, has sifted out half a dozen flies as dependable fish-takers. There will be days when nothing but the Grannom will do, but not many, and then only on the rivers where there is a big hatch of that fly. The beginner need not think of such days. Let him ask any half-dozen good Eden fishermen what are their favourite flies. Most of them will include one or two out of these three, Snipe and Yellow, Snipe and Purple, and partridge and Orange. On the Ribble, I was given a list that included these three and another eight, Winter Brown, Waterhen Bloa, Yellow Partridge, Crimson Waterhen, Iron Blue, Brown Owl, Poult Bloa and Rusty Poult. These are all standard Yorkshire flies, very lightly dressed, and will serve all over the country. But they are too many for a beginner's box. Such a boxful is direct temptation to him to spend his time in looking at it, getting dizzy, and changing flies instead of fishing. I should be inclined to tell him to keep a Greenwell on his cast and for the other two flies, ring the changes on the first three. Let him fish these until he is quite certain that the fly and not the fisherman is at fault.

This then is the sort of list I should suggest. *Dry*: March Brown, Hirst's Fancy, Wickham, Greenwell, Dunne's Black Gnat. As is right in a short list, three of these are general utility flies of different tones. Black Gnat will sometimes take trout in sunshine when all the others are useless. Hirst's Fancy floating gaily is like a good big dun. It will serve at a pinch for Mayfly. Sunk, in desperate moments, it has been taken for a little fish. March Brown is too old a favourite to be left out. *Wet*: March Brown, Greenwell, Wickham, Snipe and Yellow, Snipe and Purple, Partridge and Orange. Perhaps Alder ought not to be omitted.

The flies named are not a complete equipment. They will not enable a fisherman to attain the unattainable and to offer the trout an exact imitation of the food he is taking at the moment. But they will catch fish and there is hardly a day in the season when one or other of them will not serve. They are as many as a beginner can well become intimate with in his first year and if, with all these flies in his box, he cannot on likely days catch fish, he had better take up golf.

Wet Flies for Down-stream Fishing

To discuss down-stream fishing at all is to assume that there is more water in the rivers than there was at the beginning of the week. But droughts must come to an end and if the rains are followed by strong down-stream winds some of us will be fishing with the wind if we are to fish at all. There are days when all but heroes fish down-stream, in spite of the fanatics of up-stream fishing who point out, rightly, that down-stream flies, cast across the river and allowed to swing slowly round with the current, describe an arc with the fisherman as its centre; that no drowned fly describes such arcs while it is being washed down with the stream; and that for this reason this style of fishing is likely to fill the creel only with small hungry fish whose appetite is greater than their intelligence. The up-stream fishers have other points to make as well, but this, about the unnatural motion of the fly, seems to me to deserve a little more attention than it gets. It does not often occur to the man who, after battling for an hour or so against the wind, turns to fish down-stream that he ought to change his flies. Yet most flies are tied for up-stream fishing. That is to say they represent insects whose natural behaviour in the water is that of creatures incapable of resisting the current in any way. If these things are to be good deceivers, 'drag', even underwater 'drag', must be avoided. And 'drag' is the chief characteristic of the motion of flies describing wide arcs below the fisherman.

The first suggestion that it might be as well to experiment in special flies for down-stream fishing came from a passage on the Water Cricket in *Trout-fishing*, an entertaining and philosophic book by Mr W. Earl Hodgson, the third edition of which was published by Black in 1925. On page 16 of that work is the following story. Captain L. and Mr Hodgson had been fishing in the Great Stour from the garden of the Poet Laureate of that time. Mr Hodgson writes: 'When it was time to go in to luncheon, at Swinford Old Manor, I had only one trout. My friend had seven splendid trout, nearly a pound each, to lay out before the Poet Laureate's delighted gaze. As Captain L. had all the morning been casting down-stream and making the fly run up against the current by long pulls, this was remark-able; but the explanation, exceedingly instructive, was at hand. 'What fly?' asked our host enthusiastically. 'I don't know its name; but here it is,' answered the fisherman, taking his rod from a corner in the hall. 'Ah!' said Mr Austin, whose know-ledge of the creatures in the woodlands and the streams is unusually minute, 'the Water Cricket!' Of all the insects of which imitations are to be found in the *Book of Flies* (the illustrations to his book), the Water Cricket is, I believe, the only one that runs about on the surface of the stream. All the others, as a rule, move only as the current of the water, or that of the air, ordains.' This anecdote illustrates an admirable lecture on the advantage of not dragging flies. Mr Hodgson did not make the deduction that, if it is sometimes inevitable to drag one's fly, it is worth while to use the particular flies whose verisimilitude is least damaged by such dragging. In his *Book of Flies* the Water Cricket is the only insect given to independent motion in the water. But there are other creatures so given, and it is not difficult to make a small list of the flies which are likely to suffer least or even to be improved as fish-catchers when fished down-stream.

It is easier today than when Mr Hodgson wrote, for nymphs are a comparatively modern invention. Nymphs, even if they only rise in the water, are more given to independent motion than drowned flies. The Hardy Pale Watery Nymph is an excellent down-stream fly on slowly moving rivers. The Water Shrimp is another 'fly' whose natural eccentricities of motion make the swing of an artificial occasionally forgivable by a fish. But nymphs and shrimps are sedentary things when compared with little fish and in fast water a fly that properly represents a little fish is likely to be forgiven a sideways wriggle across the current which would make a wise trout turn in horror from an alleged fly that performed any such antics.

Of fish flies there have been quite a number, masquerading under other names. They might be Alexandra or Butcher to the fisherman, but if the trout called them fish and took a firm hold of them, it was a mistake he was always ready to condone. For some years now I have been surprised at the good fish taken by a friend with a Hirst's Fancy, even when, as sometimes happened, he fished it down-stream. Floating and cocked on the water, this fly is a good imitation of a large dun. It has even served as a Mayfly. But swinging across the stream it took good fish just the same and, on this day, as I write, I get a letter from an excellent fisherman to say that with a Hirst's Fancy (silver-bodied) he took a good trout with a little trout still in its mouth. There is the explanation. To that trout it was yet another little fish. Mr J. C. Mottram gives a very likely looking dressing for an alevin, which ought to do for down-stream fishing. I have not tried it. Teal and Green possibly looks like a little stickle-back or perch. The 'fry-fly' for which I can vouch is one in which the back and belly are sharply contrasted, white silk below and feather laid lengthwise above. I make a stoutish body of ordinary white tying silk. A few strands of red ibis and over them a few of peacock, including three or four of the brilliant blue from the eye of the tail feather, are laid along the top of this body and tied in at the head and bend of the hook. They project over the bend and are there cut to form a fan-like fin. They are cut off close at the head, which is emphasized by a number of turns of bronze peacock herl in front of a largish black cock hackle, which in the water gives the most realistic imitation of the dithering of a tiny fish. I have known a trout come at this fly, tug so that it bent the rod, lose the fly and

42

charge instantly at it again, to be duly hooked and landed. Now that is a common event in minnow fishing and seems to me to prove that one trout at any rate thought that here was a small fish trying to get away from him. Its unnatural movement in the water merely confirmed his opinion.

A keeper was with a down-stream fisherman and saw his fly pass within reach of a big trout. 'The fish came up,' said the keeper, 'swung round with the fly and then ran away from it.' Now if that fly had been a representation of something capable of moving on its own account the trout might have run away with it instead of running away from it. To meet the special case of a down-stream wind against which we are not prepared to fish all day, we should carry a match-box full of flies whose verisimilitude is enhanced instead of being destroyed by down-stream fishing. We do not need a lot. A few nymphs, a shrimp and a fry or minnow fly will do a great deal better for us than our imitations of the ephemeridae which are the more unsuitable for down-stream fishing the more closely they resemble the insects they are tied to represent.

Fishermen's Patience

Nothing is more trying to the patience of fishermen than the remark so often made to them by the profane: 'I have not patience enough for fishing.' It is not so much the remark itself (showing a complete and forgivable ignorance of angling as it does) that is annoying as the manner in which it is said, the kindly condescending manner in which Ulysses might tell Penelope that he had not patience for needlework. What are they, these dashing, impatient sparks? Are they d'Artagnans all, rough-riders, playboys of a western world, wild desperate fellows who look for a spice of danger in their pleasures? Not a bit of it. They hit a ball backwards and forwards over a net or submit to the patient trudgery of golf, a laborious form of open-air patience in which you hit a ball, walk earnestly after it and hit it again. These devotees of monotonous artificial pleasures who say that fishing is too slow a game for them seem to imagine that fishing is a sedentary occupation. Let them put on waders and fish up a full river and then walk down it on a hot summer day. Let them combine for an afternoon the arts of the Red Indian and the mountaineer and, in the intervals of crawling through brambles and clambering over boulders, keep cool enough to fill a basket with the up-stream worm. Let them discover that they have to take their coats off when salmon fishing on a day when the line freezes in the rings. Let them spin for pike in February, or trout in August. They will find that they get exercise enough. Some forms of fishing are sedentary, in the purely physical sense, in that after a man has baited a spot for carp or roach, or anchored a boat for perch, he keeps still. But he has not attained a sort of Nirvana, like a crystal gazer, isolating himself from nature by concentration

44

on a miserable ball. His mind is not dulled but lively with expectation and, of all the virtues, patience is the one he least requires. Of all kinds of fishing only one requires patience and that is trailing a bait after a boat when someone else is doing the rowing. Even in those forms of fishing which do not mean moving about, it never occurs to an angler to pride himself on his patience. Self-control, if you like, but not the most leisurely of all the virtues. There would be patience needed to watch a float which (there being no fish in the water) you knew would never budge, but none in watching a float that may at any moment make a demand for instant action.

What other people mistake for patience in anglers is really nothing of the sort but a capacity for prolonged eagerness, an unquenchable gusto in relishing an infinite series of exciting and promising moments, any one of which may yield a sudden crisis with its climax of triumph or disaster. Something rather like patience may be required by the kind of fisherman who casts a fly mechanically and uniformly and is jerked into consciousness only by some extraordinarily altruistic little trout who in a passion of benevolence hangs himself on the end of an undeserving line. But such fisherman seldom persist and, if they do persist, learn to fish in a different manner. Fishing, properly so called, is conducted under continuous tension. The mere putting of fly or bait on or in the water is an action needing skill, an action that can be done well or ill and consequently a source of pleasure. Many an angler returns with an empty basket after a day made delightful by the knowledge that he was putting his float exactly where he wanted it, casting his fly a little better than usual, or dropping his spinner with less splash at greater distances. The mere athletics of casting give the fishermen all the golfer's pleasure in good driving or putting. But, and here is the point, there is no red flag to show the angler in what direction he should aim, to take from him all initiative, to put him, as it were in blinkers. His free will is limited only by his skill in execution. If he is a trout fisher he is watching the river for a rise, for a boil, for the slight swirl in the water that betrays a fish feeding below, for the roll in the surface made by a submerged stone above which may be a motionless pocket, below which may be a minute eddy, either a fit place for a trout to lie in wait for his dinner. Now and again, if the river is new to him, he will find a hole in what he had thought was continuous shallow and will tell himself to remember next time to fish that spot before he comes to it. All the time he is watching for cover and will use the hole that he kicked himself for not seeing before he came to it to keep low and out of sight while he casts to another likely spot above. He marks where the water runs slow under the banks. At the hang of a pool he tries to put his flies at once just where the fish is likeliest to be. He knows that a mistake is all but irrevocable, that a first cast has a better chance than a second and a second a much better chance than a third. His day is a long series of crises and demands on his presence of mind. Even in float-fishing so much depends on observation, on watercraft, on the reading of barely perceptible signs, that those who imagine that a good fisherman can watch his float and think of something else beside his fishing are very much mistaken. So completely does fishing occupy a man that if a good angler had murdered one of those people who prate about patience and were allowed to spend his last day at the river instead of in the condemned cell, he would forget the rope.

The ultimate test is one of time. Patience is a virtue required when time goes slowly. In fishing time goes too fast. Fishermen's wives are unanimous in deploring the hopeless unpunctuality of their husbands at the fag-end of the day. Fishermen rarely have time to eat all the sandwiches provided for their luncheons. If, on occasion, they do eat in leisure at the waterside it is with the peculiar relish that accompanies stolen fruit. They run a race with the sun, and are always finding that it has beaten them and is casting their shadow on the water long before they had expected to have to cross the river. The only time that seems to the fishermen longer than it is is that in which he is playing a big fish. Then, indeed, his drawn-out anxiety makes him apt to think he spent an hour in landing a salmon which was actually on the bank in fifteen minutes. But no one will suggest that those minutes were so dull that they needed to be patiently borne.

The Morality of 'Nymphs'

Writing in 1905, Mr W. M. Gallichan (in his *Fishing in Derbyshire*) mentioned that John Fosbrooke, who used to fish the Manifold with the wet fly, was tying 'some quaint and killing patterns, much resembling the insect as it emerges from the pupa'. During the last few years a number of fishermen have been experimenting along just these lines, and tying flies in deliberate imitation of the insects on which the trout feeds, not in the form in which they are usually obvious to ourselves but in that earlier stage of their development in which they come to the notice of the fish while still submerged. Farlows, Ogden Smiths, and Hardys all sell their own patterns of these 'nymphs', and it is interesting to notice that a wet-fly fisherman can usually, on looking at one of these new creations, name a standard wet fly which, in colour at least, resembles it. The difference is in shape. It is not extravagant to suppose that those wet flies were taken by the trout because of their resemblance to nymphs, and that their makers were doing by accident what the makers of the new nymphs are doing on purpose. That there has been an advance in fidelity to nature is almost proved by the success of the nymphs on chalk streams where hitherto, if there was nothing doing with the dry fly, there was nothing doing at all. The innovation has, of course, been met with hints of heresy and worse. I was given an example last week.

There were occasional duns on the water, but no rises. In the patch of smooth, clear water below a clump of weeds a fish was signalling by repeated flashes that, although he never broke the surface, he was busy with his dinner. There were two fishermen considering the stream. One of them (the more

skilful) mounted a large winged, silver-bodied dun, and persisted with it or with other winged flies of similar size. The
other offered the feeding fish a small floating fly, then another,
and, when these were refused, a pale grey nymph on a cast
greased to within six inches of the end. The nymph was taken
below the surface, but so near it as to cause a violent splash,
and when the fish was landed the fly was found to be well back
in its mouth. On that the fisherman reasoned that he had found
something sufficiently near the trout's menu for that day to be
taken with confidence. He kept the pale grey nymph on his
cast, and at three or four o'clock, when he trudged through
the water meadows to meet his companion for a late luncheon,
he had eleven trout in his bag. He had landed and returned
perhaps half that number of smaller fish. His companion had
risen and landed on his big floating fly a good many small fish,
but had not caught any fit for the basket. Two other fishermen,
fishing similar large duns on a lower beat of the same water,
had got a couple of fish apiece. In the absence of the fortunate
fisherman there ensued an indignation meeting on the subject
of the morality of nymphs.

'He got them fishing with a thing you could not call a fly.'

'You might almost call it a grub.'

'It was not floating.'

'Why not use worm?'

These remarks were reported to the fortunate fisherman
when, going out again at five o'clock, in half an hour's fishing
he raised his total to fourteen, while his companion, admittedly
a more skilful fisherman, landed his first sizeable fish that day,
while rising and landing any quantity of the undersized. The
nymph fisherman in self-defence produced his fly. It was tied
on a small hook. It had a bit of a hump at one end of the body
and at the head of it two considerable tufts of hackle projected
horizontally on either side. The fly was a Hardy fly, described
by its makers as a 'Pale Watery Nymph.'

The fisher of the nymph *loquitur*; 'Will you please explain to me why a hook with tufts of feathers fastened on in the shape of a V is considered admirable, while one with tufts of feathers set horizontally is so shocking?'

Companion: 'A wingless fly is as much of a contradiction in terms as a two-legged quadruped. You have been fishing with a grub instead of with a fly.'

'Come, come. We have neither of us been fishing with either flies or grubs but with hooks decorated with scraps of feathers. The difference is simply in the angle at which the feathers are worn by the hook, the cock of a bonnet, in fact. The object of the feathers on the hook is to suggest to the trout that the combined hook and feathers is something worth eating. It rather looks as if today the thing the trout are eating is better suggested by horizontal than vertical feathers, that is all. Your fly is my fly wearing a different fashion, and I have no doubt that on another day, if the trout were feeding on the surface, you would catch fourteen with your fly to my one with the nymph, except that on that day my nymphs would remain in their box and I should be using a fly resembling as nearly as possible whatever insect it was that I could see the trout were picking off the surface. After all, you do not consider it immoral to fish with, for example, a Jenny Spinner. Now you can see, if you will be good enough to look at one, that a properly tied spinner wears its feathers in a fashion precisely like that which is followed by my nymph.'

'But you fish the spinner on the surface.'

'And I fish the nymph just below the surface. Not that, if I saw that the trout were grubbing on the bottom, I should not try to meet that preference also. Today, every fish I caught broke the surface as he took the fly. On another day he might not. But you have now shifted your ground and complain of the morality of my poor nymph, not because of the way she does her hair, but because she has not been dipped in oil and made to float.'

There was a good deal more said on both sides, but neither

of the disputants seemed to get at the root of the matter. Surely the origin of dry-fly fishing was the discovery that it was possible to catch with a floating fly fish that were not to be tempted by a fly submerged. The men who began to make a practice of fishing their flies floating did not do so by way of handicapping themselves because they had been catching too many fish. Quite the reverse. And to lay down the rule that a fish caught by a wet fly is a fish immorally caught is to restrict that adaptability to circumstance which is the pride of a good fishermen. If we are not to adapt our presentation of the fly to the manner in which the trout are feeding, we may as well go a step further and cease to vary our flies according to those we observe on the water. We may as well have a standard fly, and, fishing nothing else, narrow still further the scope of our observation and ingenuity.

On Watching Fishermen

If I am walking with a man and we pass an urchin fishing with a bent pin in a ditch and my companion is unwilling to linger, I suspect that he is a poor specimen of a human being and I am certain that he is no fisherman. In any case, I should not be keen to go for a walk with him again. I should feel for him the same resentment that I felt for the liner in the Bay of Biscay that carried me all too fast past the tunny-fisher with his huge fishing rods hinged to the foot of his mast while, looking back through glasses, I hoped and hoped, till the tunny-fisher was a blob on the horizon, that I should see that seventy-foot rod flutter and spring under the tugs of a gigantic fish. Out of many years of travel, the moments that need least remembering, because their detail is still as bright and clear as when it was first burnt into my mind, are the moments spent in watching fishermen. I think of the Arab with his long bamboo whom I watched till dusk catching mullet (I think) in the harbour of Alexandria; of the workman in Petrograd, sitting on the stern-post of a barge in the Neva, fishing for perch while the revolution was noisily proceeding in the town; of waking at night during a long journey with post-horses and seeing the yellow flashing of the torches carried by the fish-spearers in the river; of the eel-fisher in a Riga canal who held me for an hour when I should have been hurrying back to my little ship with the stores for which I had come ashore; of the rows of long rods dangled perpendicularly downwards from the embankments of the Seine; of the sheepskin-coated, felt-booted crowd fishing through the ice under the Kremlin walls; and of that spectacle that welcomes the returning traveller, that row of men in oilskins who seem to fish in all weathers from the piers of Dover harbour.

I am never likely to do any netting, but I cannot see a net being drawn without waiting to see what is in it. How much more difficult do I find it to move on when I have come across a fisherman using rod and line. Another man's float will satisfy me for hours. Most interesting of all is it to watch the fly-fisher. It is interesting and, I fancy, unnecessarily humbling. Watching an angler is like reading the biography of a man whose life in some way closely resembles our own. We do not often assume equality with him. It is very seldom that we watch a fisherman who seems to cast as badly as we know we sometimes cast ourselves. Nearly always the watched fisherman seems to cast with enviable skill. That is because only the trout is as conscious as the actual fisherman of the bungled cast and the splash of the line in the water. The observer on the bridge sees the general movement, not the detail. He sees the line lift, fly back and, coming forward, unroll itself with easy precision. The thing seems a miracle and yet, in nine cases out of ten, observer and fisherman could change places without affecting the impression made. Criticism is usually not of the casting but of the fisherman's use of his obvious, astonishing skill. The observer, looking at the river, knows just where, if he were fishing it, he would wish the fly to alight. The fisherman omits to send it into just that place. I remember watching one of the most skilful casters and worst fishermen I have ever seen. His action was beautiful, effortless, rhythmic with never a jerk, never a tussle with one of those jack-in-the-box hawthorn bushes that were not there when we looked round, but bob up out of the earth just in time to catch our fly. But cast after cast dropped his fly perfectly on precisely those spots where, un-less by the accident of travel, no trout would ever be. This fisherman chose the places where the trout lay, not to fish over but to stand in. I have never seen a more delicate or a more unprofitable performance. And then I remember watching another man who, though his casting was not pretty to watch, always managed to get his share of fish. Again and again he would pick up a trout from a place I should certainly have passed over, though, after he had taken a trout from it, it was easy to see just why it was a proper station for a feeding fish. Both these men were worth watching. There was something to learn from them. But, if they had been simply down-stream raking with wet flies, I should have watched them just the same. There is no need for any sordid utilitarian excuse for doing what we should do whether we hoped to profit by it or not. Fishing of any kind is to the fisherman one of the vividest forms of life and other fishermen watch him and live vicariously in so doing, much as we intensify our consciousness of existence by going to the play. We share his excitement and, so primitive are we in this matter that we are apt, at the great moments (when he has a good fish on) to shout advice from the gallery. It is only the man who is himself highly developed as a fisherman who can refrain at such moments from seeking to thrust himself from among the audience upon the stage itself.

Fishermen are those who get most out of watching other people fish. But they are not the only folk who watch them. Nearly everybody does. Everybody, I should say, except those who have been thoroughly disheartened by life. Even old ladies who do not know salmon from cod except when boiled, cannot tear themselves away from the bridge. The sight of a man running towards a railway station makes people stop and wonder if he will catch his train. But this interest is mild and colourless compared to that with which on seeing an angler they will neglect all duties to watch if he will catch a fish. The train is hidden by nothing more mysterious than the bricks and mortar of the railway station. Also the catching of a train is something calculable. Even the biggest trains do not elude us, if we take our seats in time. Not so with the fish. He is in another element and the fisherman, plain to view, is fishing as it were into the fourth dimension, into the unknown. This, perhaps, explains his universal interest for other men. He shares the wondering interest (veiled sometimes in a joke), with which men stare after philosophers. The philosopher is sometimes unrecognized, because he does not wear a Druidic robe or carry a fishing rod to show that he is seeking to cozen something out of the unknown. The fisherman cannot disguise himself and everyone who sees what he is about must stop, if only for a moment, to see what he gets out of it, or if, as so often happens, he does not get anything at all.

I hope I shall remember all these reasons for forgiveness, the next time that, after I have laboriously crawled within casting distance of the big trout under the bridge, a group of spectators appear on the parapet and, pointing out with parasols both fisherman and quarry, send the one to shelter and the other to seek some other fish to stalk.

Mayflies and Mayflies

In the south, when men speak of Mayflies, you know what they mean, the Green Drakes, Grey Drakes and subsequent Spent Gnats that, golloped down so greedily by the trout, make the Mayfly season a sort of annual Bounty to the fisherman and, no doubt, were in Sir Henry Wotton's mind when he exclaimed that 'he would rather have five May months than forty Decembers'. It was the adoption of the new calendar that brought most of the Mayfly fishing into June. In the north we have these Mayflies too in some places, but when the north-country fisherman says that the Mayfly is up, you must ask yourself what are the waters he fishes, for he is likely to mean not the Green Drake but the Stone-fly which, though up here it shares the Mayfly's name, is unlike it in every respect save two, its size and its peremptory interest to the trout.

The Stone-fly, says the fisherman of Ripon, Michael Theakston, 'is the head of her class, and the Imperial Empress of all trout flies; her size and nutritious qualities, whereof the trout feeds to satiety, and it is said perfects his condition, has no equal. Her name is famous among anglers; but few arrive to the extent of her merits. . . . It might seem that our great Creator, amidst his animated masses, threw in the sequestered devoted Stone-fly a peck for the trout, as the burnisher of his beauties and his chief nourisher in life's feast.' Theakston has a dressing for the female Stone-fly (usually preferred): 'Body of yellow camlet, with eight or nine rounds of brown floss silk, or camlet thread warpt over it; head and shoulders yellow camlet, darkened on the upper parts, etcetera, with the brown bear's hair; wings selected from the feathers of a wild drake, partridge, or hen pheasant; legged with hair or a stiff hen hackle.' He means mohair by 'camlet' which, the Oxford Dictionary says, was originally 'a costly Eastern stuff of silk and camel's hair,' no doubt fitting for an Imperial Empress. In these modern, republicanish days we have come down from camlet and bearskin to dubbing of water rat and hare, but in other respects we follow Theakston's dressing, using hen pheasant wing feathers for the wings. We give it whisks of mallard or pheasant. At this time, on the rivers where it abounds, it is a bad fly to be without. When trout are taking it they will seldom interest themselves in any other.

Two years ago, in mid-May, the summer was showing signs of coming in. Damson blossom had fallen and apple-blossom was full in the orchards by the river. The new oak leaves showed golden orange against the rocks. Even the ash-buds were opening. I had stopped a moment by the lake on my way to the river and a sandpiper had scuttered away over the ground and in her anxiety shown me where two pointed, mottled eggs lay hardly hidden by a frond of bracken and some bluebell leaves. In the meadow by the river-side I heard the corncrake and took his cheerful noise as a sign that it might be worth while waiting for the evening rise. It was. I doubled my day's basket in an hour by throwing an Alder and a March Brown with the wings cut off to trout busily rising. It was not the evening rise of full summer when, at sundown, the trout make the quiet stretches of the river boil with their rises. It was too early for that. But it was a definite 'time of the take' coming late in the day. At the beginning of the season, especially in the north, the angler seldom has this second chance after the fish have done with rising through the middle, warmer parts of cold spring days. It was closely connected with the Stone-fly. Let me explain how it was that my evening cast carried a March Brown severely trimmed at the riverside.

On coming to the river on that pleasant day I had not at first suspected that the reason why the trout were taking no notice of the upwinged flies that were on the water was that they had already become interested in the Imperial Empress. I had begun fishing, carelessly, with a cast that was already made up, of which the middle fly was a Woodstock and Orange. Thanks to this fly I was bothered by parr and smolts (in their new silver coats, ready for the sea). I took it off to discourage them and put on instead a lightly built Stone-fly, with the wings lying flat along the shank of the hook. I put it on for no sound reason. I had not seen a Stone-fly and I put this one on the cast out of sheer light-heartedness, a salute to the warm weather, like humming the first bars of 'Summer is i-cumen in'. The trout had been waiting for nothing else. I had begun to think I was sure of a good basket when, after making the Stone-fly the stretcher, as its performance deserved, I forgot to look behind me in eagerness to reach a promising, difficult corner and left it in the topmost branch of a hawthorn tree. I was lucky to recover most of the cast. There was nothing for it but to sit on the bank and put on some fresh lengths of gut from the tobacco pouch while considering the mixed charm and obduracy of hawthorns. It was not until this was done that I looked in my box and found that I had not another Stone-fly in it. I tried in turn one flat-winged fly after another. No. The shape was right but not the colour. I began to take fish again when I put on an Alder, but I had no confidence in it and the fish were taking it more out of politeness than eagerness. Presently there came on a violent downpour of rain and hail and they went off altogether and so did I. This splash of winter passed and the sun shone out again. It occurred to me that I had a dark March Brown that might deceive these trout. It did not. The colour was not far wrong, but the shape was preposterous. I cut off its wings and some of its hackle, trimming it as well as I could to Stone-fly shape, and whether it was that or the return of warmth, a few trout decided that it was near enough to the Stone-fly to be worth trying. Then they stopped and, marvelling at the flies on the water and the absence of rising fish, I ate my sandwiches and was on the point of starting for home when the corncrake put me in the mood to wait. Evening and early morning are the Stone-fly's time, and sitting on the bank under the trees I had not long to wait. First one, then another, then half a dozen fish together stirred the smooth water and I slipped quietly down. They now took the mutilated March Brown and the Alder as if they meant it and let me leave off with the fish I wanted while they were still rising. They were kind to accept these substitutes, but they had taught me never again to go wet fly-fishing on this river after the first of May without a respectable supply of Stone-flies in my box.

The local fishermen hardly ever use the artificial Stone-fly. It was so in Theakston's day. He says, 'The Stone-fly is in general fished natural, for which herself, like all others, is the best teacher,' and points out one essential difference between this May-fly and the other, in that, whereas the Drake is usually passive except on the wing, the Stone-fly runs across the surface of the water. This, like the Water Cricket, is a fly in the fishing of which 'drag' is no betrayal of the angler but adds to the confidence of the trout, unless the drag is of such a kind as to bring the fly up against the current. One good fisherman I knew who used to fish the artificial Stone-fly as top dropper instead of as stretcher, in order the better to imitate the irregular motions of the insect on the skin of the water. The best way of learning how to fish the artificial Stone-fly is, if the insect herself does not teach you, to copy the methods of those who fish the natural. They suggest one or two variations from usual practice.

There is a special art of Stone-fly fishing, in which the late Mr Nelson was a master. It is divided into two branches, the fishing of the Creeper or Stone-fly nymph and the fishing of the Stone-fly proper. Some of the local men expect their best baskets from the one, some from the other. The secret of both branches is to fish in the right place. Creepers may be caught by the trout at any stage of their migration from the river to the shore. The trout have been known to turn stones for them, but expect them to come tumbling down in the fast water. The fly, however, hatches on dry land and the trout waits for it where land and water meet and at one other place, which in the smaller rivers, is the more profitable to the fisherman. A slight rise of water washes the flies from the stones at the water's edge and the fisherman moving up-stream fishes just here, where, sometimes, the trout are as if in single file waiting for the insects. But in the small rivers and the becks, there is no room for this careful fishing of the thin edges of the stream. The pools are short and close together, the stream swift, and the proper fishing of the Stone-fly has a different character. Here too the fisherman likes a rise of water to wet the harbour- ing places of the fly, but both the trout and he gather their harvest at the heads of the pools. On one small river I know, water is released on certain days at certain times from a dam for the working of a mill. The water rises for an hour or two and at the right season of the year gathers with it the Stone- flies on the water's edge and invites the trout to feed. The trout respond by taking their places in the narrow neck of every tiny pool. The gathered Stone-flies are concentrated and swept down through these necks and the local fisher of the natural fly catches the trout by letting his insect come sweeping through the neck of the pool like any other. In this tiny river there is no room for the delicate side-swing casts of Eden and Eamont. The method here is to dap. The fisherman, in the oldest clothes he has, works through the brambles to a position from which he can bring the tip of his rod over the rough water in the neck of a pool. His line is adjusted anew for each place. In one he will use a line as long as his rod, in another he must use a longer and throw his fly, but mostly his line is shorter than his rod and unweighted. He daps the fly on the fast water, following it down a foot or two, but never letting it be carried under. The fish come up hard at it, are hooked without pre- cipitation, lifted from the water and got somehow or other into the fisherman's possession. A net in these thickets would be a terrible encumbrance for as long as it lasted, which would not be long. It is often impossible to lift the rod because of boughs overhead. Two or even three trout may be tricked from each such stickle and these being the best places they will be the best fish. If a second trout does not at once follow the first, the fisherman hardens his heart to bramble scratches and works up to the next pool. Yesterday I met in the evening a friend and local fisherman back from an evening's fishing. He had noticed that the Stone-fly was about, collected a boxful and then sat down to wait till the dam should be opened, before beginning to fish. He tied a couple of tackles (two hooks one above another, facing opposite ways) while keeping his eye on a stone at the water's edge. As soon as he saw the water rising over the stone, he set off upstream, at four in the afternoon. By seven o'clock he was back with thirty-two in his pannier, all good fish for this little river. 'There's nothing like the May-fly,' said he, emptying his pannier before the eyes of envy. Well, we cannot do as well as that with the artificial, but, by taking the Imperial Empress as our teacher, fishing the stony edges at dusk, if the river is not rising, throughout the day if it is, and in smaller rivers, fishing the heads of the little pools, we can do well enough with this, our northern Mayfly, to console ourselves if our water is without the Green Drake.

Fish and the Eclipse

Fish, during the eclipse, were rather disappointing. Their reactions to it were entirely negative, and as, both before and after the eclipse, their positive activity was not great, such difference in behaviour as was caused in them by the eclipse was less noticeable than it might have been. During previous eclipses it had been observed that cattle stopped feeding and that birds, mistaking the approaching shadow for evening, flew to their roosting places. Hens are said to be much worried by such phenomena. I had a sort of hope that fish would show their feelings in some remarkable way, and, in spite of previous testimony on the behaviour of animals of other kinds, had somehow allowed the optimism that is as important to the fisherman as his line to persuade me that the trout would show their interest by coming to the top of the water. I had thought that the Astronomers-Royal of the Fish would be about in prominent places, and that I might catch one and put him in a glass case with a diagram of the obscured sun. I could find no mention of the effect of the eclipse on fish, but if cattle stopped feeding that would not necessarily mean that fish would do the same, and if birds flew to their roosting places that would seem to mean that they thought night was upon them, and, if fish should reason in the same way, there might at 6.24 in the morning of 29 June (1927) be a very satisfactory Evening Rise.

In any case, it was my business to go and see, so I broke all rules by being on the water of the tarn at 5.30 in the morning, thinking that, as there is to be no other such eclipse for some seventy years, I was not likely to break the rules in this way again, and could almost count on being forgiven for a first offence. In the valley I had left great quantities of human

62

beings who were being affected by the eclipse in different ways. Between Settle and this place, at that early hour, I had heard mouth organs, accordions, and at least one brass band. I had seen men walking up the hills as fast as if they wished to escape the shadow. I had seen other men practising for looking at the sun by looking through smoked glass at the young women who accompanied them. I had, however, seen that a great many people were making use of the eclipse for their own livelihood. They were trying to entice motor-cars into fields for their own profit. They were, at this unusual time, doing a roaring trade in lemonade and petrol. The eclipse was giving them an improved chance of making a living, and they were grabbing at that chance with both hands. The fish, I thought, would probably do the same. But, just then, I saw a ginger cat going home in the dawn and remembered that, whereas the human beings had foreknowledge of the coming shadow, the cat had none, or it would have lurked out in the fields to spring in the shadow of the moon on a startled rabbit. The trout would be like the cat, not like the human beings, in that the darkness and the shadow would come up upon them unawares.

A flock of geese moved protesting from the tarn as I arrived. It was, of course, quite light. There was hardly a breath of wind. Here and there were quiet rings on the water. There were big clouds over the Yorkshire hills, but among them open spaces dazzling with the glow of the rising sun. I put up my rod with the sort of cast that I should put up for an evening rise and, with an occasional pull at the oars to help, drifted down the tarn, wetting my flies as I drifted and wondering what it was the fish were taking, seemingly close under but not on the surface of the water. (I found out, after I had packed up to go away, that they were taking swimming nymphs.) It was very cold, and I landed and looked for a meadow pipit's nest and walked to keep warm. At 5.40 I saw a good splashing rise and a fish come half out of water. The sun showed through the clouds like a brass saucer out of which some mad hatter had taken a bite. A wind came up. I pulled into the middle of the tarn. Fish were still feeding, and I caught a small one under half a pound who went back, not to be deprived of the experience that was coming, but, though coming so soon, was so little foreshadowed. The light was waning, but not much more noticeably than it often does under a thunder-cloud. The geese, up on the hillside, moved off rapidly. Three human beings showed on the skyline far above me. The sheep stopped feeding and moved restlessly about in little groups. Fish still rose. Then the speed of events seemed to quicken. Everything went suddenly dark. The noise of curlews, peewits, and small upland birds stopped. There was absolute silence, and it was as if a roof had suddenly been put over the tarn. I had a glimpse of the shrouded sun, but no attention for it, casting carefully in places where a few moments before the fish had been rising, and watching and listening for the movement of a fish. The tarn was dead. I saw no rise and heard no rise. It was exactly like fishing a pool in a river over which a fisherman has inadvertently moved his own shadow. That, I think, is what the eclipse seemed to the trout. It was the sudden passing of a tremendous shadow, the shadow not of a cloud but of a solid body, and they reacted to it exactly as they would to the shadow of a rod or a fisherman, and buried themselves in the weeds or the deepest water.

The shadow passed and the tarn was again in daylight, but it was twenty minutes later that I saw the first fish rise. I drifted down on him, and, getting my flies over him just where he had risen beside a weed bed, had him in the boat a minute or two later, a small fish just over the limit. He was presently followed by a smaller one just under the limit, who went back. After that, the morning of the eclipse was an ordinary fishing morning and one of the worst. I could not rise many fish and I could catch none. One hooked himself in the tail and escaped by taking out thirty yards of line and bolting into a reed bed. Another, hooked on the dropper, caught the tail fly in the weeds and so freed himself. I was very sleepy and was startled by the only good fish I met, who went off with half a cast and two of my best flies, tied specially for the eclipse. These things, unsatisfactory in themselves, were, however, enough to prove that trout, feeding normally before the eclipse, stopped feeding altogether at the passage of the moon's shadow, ceased to feed for about as long as when put down by the shadow of a careless fisherman, and, plucking up heart with the second dawn that day, resumed their feeding. All of which was precisely what might have been expected.

The Dry-fly Strike

Most disagreements are caused by the disputants using the same word to mean different things. This is particularly noticeable when the subject of dispute is one of the comparative speeds. The racing tortoise hardly seems to the hare to be hurrying. What is quick to the one is decidedly slow to the other. It is for reasons of this kind that good fishermen give such contradictory advice about striking. Fishermen differ from each other and so do fishing rods, and absolute speed in striking depends on man and rod as well as on the intention of one in using the other. A first-rate fisherman questioned on this point, said that, in grayling fishing, he tries to strike when he sees the grayling rising through the water to take his floating fly. I asked him, expecting a different reply, when he thought a man should strike on getting a rise from a trout. He replied that with them, too, his only care was to strike quickly enough. This, for some moments, made me suspect that he was one whose nerves obeyed an impulse slowly. I then remembered that he fished with an old-fashioned rod, decidedly soft in comparison with the stiff rods mostly used for dry-fly fishing today. Now, with a whippy rod, there is a much longer interval between the angler's impulse to the rod and the resultant tightening of the line. The first movement of the top of the rod actually slackens instead of tightening the line. A fisherman using such a rod would certainly have to strike sooner than if he were using a stiff one.

Centuries of whippy rods and centuries of wet-fly fishing combine to explain why spectators always make the same comment when a fisherman misses a trout that has risen at his fly. That comment is, 'You did not strike quick enough.' Now when a trout takes a fly under water the disturbance he makes on the surface (if he makes any disturbance at all) is nearly always an indication that he has already taken the fly. The 'wink under water' described by Mr Skues is an indication of the same thing. The actual pluck at the line is, even more obviously, not made by a trout before the fly is in his mouth. In fact almost all indications that a trout is concerned with the fly are, in wet-fly fishing, indications that the angler had better lose no time before tightening on the line. His speed in doing this is lessened by the character of the rod usually employed for fishing wet-fly. He has very good reason for believing that when he misses a fish it is because he has been too late.

On the other hand, the commotion on the surface made by a fish taking a floating fly is made either before or at the moment he takes the fly into his mouth. The nervous fisherman, accustomed to wet flies and to a whippy rod, who tightens the moment he sees the surface of the water break, misses his fish not because he has struck too late but because he has struck too soon. It does not comfort him, as he adjures himself to give the next one time, to hear the spectator announce that he did not strike quick enough. The most obvious example is the head and tail rise, when the fish comes out of the water and, descending head first, takes the fly with it. It is clearly useless, with such a rise, to strike before the fish is going down. And how difficult it is, at that violent and beautiful apparition, to refrain. But take the more debatable case, when the trout comes up quietly and the fly disappears in a ring. Consider what happens when it is possible, as it often is, to watch the fish before, during and after its rising. Seeing the fish, the angler puts his fly in the right position to float if not over it then a little to one side. He sees first a slight, indescribable change in the aspect of the fish, possibly a minute change of position, showing that it notices the fly. He then sees the fish slant upwards while being carried backwards by the current so that fish and fly meet at the surface an inch or two below the point at which the fish was lying. The fish then turns down and forward to regain its original position. With such a rise, a tightening of the line that coincides with or immediately follows the breaking of the surface of the water will not hook the fish, in 99 cases out of 100. In a great many cases a tightening of the line delayed until the trout has returned to its position after taking the fly will hook it securely. These are the extremes. Somewhere between them must be the moment to be aimed at, at which the greatest number of strikes will be successful. One thing is certain; that at the moment of breaking the surface, the moment of the 'rise', the trout's mouth is open and, even if the fly is in it, it is likely to be removed from it by any tightening of the line. We do not know when the trout closes its mouth, but, by the time that it is on the forward, downward journey it is likely to have a less insecure hold of the fly. With large fish and large flies the advantage of delay in striking is generally admitted by dry-fly fishermen, most of whom agree that there is no need for hurry even with a small fly. With smaller fish we are often told that it is necessary to strike sooner. Experiment is very difficult, because it is not easy to find a number of fish to rise from the same depth on the same day in the same manner. But after a number of experiments with small fish I am inclined to think that it is not the size of the fish that should influence the fisherman in deciding when to strike but the speed of the water. In slow water I found it as easy to miss fingerlings by quick striking as to miss pounders. In fast water, the action of the fish is quicker, presumably because, if it were not, his flies would cost him more in the energy he must spend in order to regain his position. The quicker he is the less he is swept down by the stream as he rises to meet the fly. In fast water the pull of the stream on the gut gives earlier warning to the fish that he has something unnatural in his mouth. It is therefore advisable not to give him so long to consider it. On the other hand, that same pull of the stream is sometimes enough to hook the fish without effort on the part of the fisherman. In any case it is better to miss a fish by striking too late than by striking too soon. If you remove a fly that a fish has already rejected, he may remain where he is to consider another fly that you may offer him a minute or two later. If you snatch a fly out of his mouth he is likely to postpone the ending of his meal until a time when he can be sure that no such ill-mannered hooligans are about. But, for the reasons mentioned at the beginning of this article, it is useless for one fisherman to tell another when to strike. One ingenious author says, 'The normal time is given by saying "One thousand, two thousand, three thousand, strike." ' by he adds, 'the timing varies on different streams.' It varies also with different men and with the different rods they use. When a man says that he finds that he hooks more fish with one rod than with another, it often means, not that one rod is better but that its action happens to correct his speed in striking which may be too fast or too slow.

Back to the Stone Age?

'A frank resumption of palaeolithic life without the spur of palaeolithic hunger.' So Mr Graham Wallas in his good book on *Human Nature in Politics* describes hunting and fishing. He does not mean it as praise. Huntsmen must make their own defence. Fishermen need question only the tone in which the words are used, for the actual words offer a profounder justification of fishing than is offered by most professed apologists. They do not mean a resumption of Stone Age barbarity. Mr Wallas wrote the words in 1920 when this age of flying machines, big guns, poison-gas, cheap newspapers and other means of creating and justifying hate and panic had only recently given proof of barbarity on such a scale as had never been equalled in the history of man. We have no need to return to the Stone Age to look for barbarity. We have enough and to spare. But it is true that fishing allows us to refresh ourselves by a temporary resumption of a life in which a man's chief concern is not inextricably confounded with other men's activities, but is, simply, to trick a dinner out of the river. The packet of sandwiches in his pocket, his possible dislike of eating fish, does not affect this matter in the least. Mr Wallas is right. We have no need for the spur of palaeolithic hunger. Our fishing satisfies quite another need. Escaping to the Stone Age by the morning train from Manchester, the fisherman engages in an activity that allows him to shed the centuries as a dog shakes off water and to recapture not his own youth merely but the youth of the world.

He may not know that this is his aim. Indeed if he were too conscious of it he would not be able to achieve it. But, if we watch him we notice a number of signs that show clearly

70

enough that when he goes fishing his primary reason is not the
need of fish. He imposes on himself unwritten laws that betray
his real intention. He has a better reason than hunger for being
a fisherman. He is not moved by a primitive instinct for
slaughter. If he were he could satisfy it better by using a hand-
grenade, poison or a net. His unwritten laws give the fish
approximately the same chance that they had against the
hungry savage. Most fishermen are secretly dissatisfied with
themselves if they feel that they owe too much of their success
to the mechanical perfection of their equipment. For example,
I have yet to meet a man who has done much spinning and fly-
fishing who would not agree at once that he would rather catch
his two-pounder on a fly than with the help of one of the
ingenious modern spinning reels. The fisherman sets the
highest value on those fish which have made the highest
demands on his personal prowess, his knowledge of nature, his
watercraft and his skill. A fish caught on a home-made fly is a
greater satisfaction to the fisherman than one which has been
tricked by a fly bought in a shop. Why? Because it better
satisfies the fisherman's instinctive desire to re-create conditions in which he depends on himself alone in his voluntary
contest with nature. There is no hostility in this contest. The
trout chasing minnows or picking flies from the surface of the
stream is contesting with Nature in the same way as the fisherman chasing trout. Neither trout nor fisherman are opposed
to Nature in their several activities. Quite the contrary. The
home-made fly gives the fisherman a better right to say,
'Alone I did it.' That is why he prefers it. We should like to
make our own rods, our own lines, if we could. But we must
make some concessions to our modern inefficiency. We can
comfort ourselves with the thought that probably even the
Stone Age Halford borrowed his cousin's rod if it was better
than his own and employed his wife's fingers in plaiting his
horsehair line.

There may have been no horsehair lines in the Stone Age.

There may even have been no rods. No matter. Mr Wallas slammed the big word palaeolithic at us not because he had any particular period in mind but because of the handy weight of its five syllables. We return in fishing not to the Stone but to the Golden Age. Historical accuracy is happily denied to us. We do not feel it necessary to go fishing in a wolf's skin instead of in a Burberry. The character of our return to this mythical age is far deeper than can be expressed by any fancy dress. What we are doing is to exchange an elaborate and indirect for a simple and direct relationship with Nature. This latter relationship is very hard to put into words. Is the fisherman returning to the Golden Age to enjoy aptitudes in himself which he might otherwise lose? Is he reassuring himself by happy experiment that he can still climb *down* his family tree? Fishing cannot be explained simply as a means of escape from our over-elaborate life, for it is enjoyed by men who have lived all their lives on the river bank as well as by those who escape to their fishing from the towns. The happiness of Walton's fishing was as keen as our own, but the country was then at a Londoner's back door. The truth, I think, is, that we resume 'palaeolithic life' not because of preference for any past age but to seek a relationship with Nature which is valuable in all ages. When William Basse wrote:

> 'My hand alone my work can do,
> So I can fish and study too'

he was either a liar or a bad fisherman. For the good fisherman is always engaged in the active exercise of his imagination. He is the fish he catches. He, as that fish, feels the currents in the pool and pushes his way to shelter in a pocket of still water. The fish that go into his creel are so many testimonials to his right reading of nature. The power of vision that he develops while fishing persists when the rod is in its case. The fisherman knows what is happening in the river when he is not there. As the rain pours down on autumn streets, he is conscious, as he buttons his coat about his neck, of the fish running up the Eden from the Solway Firth. The pavements are soft grass under his feet, the stone walls of the houses are no prison for him and through the roar of the towns he can hear running water. It is this that distinguishes fishing from such pursuits as golf, cricket, football, billiards, or chess. These games do not affect a man's relationship to nature. Fishing does. In looking round for another pursuit of which this can be said, I think of gardening. The gardener, like the fisherman, 'resumes palaeolithic life without the spur of palaeolithic hunger.' Like the fisherman he becomes so much a part of Nature that he is reconciled to the changes of the year. He welcomes the seasons as they come and no longer wishes to put a spoke in the wheel of time. It is generally said that gardeners and fishermen make fine old men. This is not surprising. They have been caught up into Nature, grow old with a good will and no hanging back, and are without misgivings about their own mortality.

The Element of Surprise

The salmon who rises to a gold-ribbed March Brown or a Butcher on a No. 1 or No. 2 hook thrown into the water to tempt his cousins the trout gives the fisherman the sort of surprise that a man gets when a friend coming up behind him thumps him on the back while he is thinking of something else. It is a crude surprise, scarcely to be recognized for the emotion that plays so large a part in the fishing of every day. Surprise is one of the qualities of every rise. Sometimes it is unmixed, as when a trout takes hold just as you withdraw your flies from the water. Sometimes it is violent, as when the salmon takes your trout-fly. In both these cases the effect on the fisherman is one of momentary paralysis, and fish that bring with their rise surprise in this degree either hook themselves or are not hooked at all. But more often the surprise that accompanies a fish laying hold is to be described, by a contradiction in terms, as expected, like a filled stocking on Christmas morning. Its most perfect form is experienced when a floating fly passes over the spot where the fish last rose and a brown nose pokes up and goes down with it at exactly that point. You expected the fly to be taken there and it is taken, but you are surprised all the same. Half the pleasure of fishing comes from the uncertainty of your reaction to that sudden crystallization of emotions held as it were in suspense. If there were no surprise at all you could count on yourself and hook your fish with almost mechanical certainty, and, having got so far, you would give up fishing and look for something more exciting. The dry-fly fisherman of the books is really an epicure in surprise. He has so far refined his fishing as to reject as crude all but this delicate Christmas stocking, promise-keeping kind of surprise.

The Element of Surprise

He looks for his big fish and puts his fly over it. He never casts but to a fish which has shown that it is there and feeding. What he would do if affronted by the onslaught of an unexpected salmon I hardly know. He would probably hand his rod to the keeper. We, in the North, have more catholic appetites. We 'fish the rise' but also 'fish the stream' without waiting to know what is in it. We make ourlseves liable to the surprise of a fish's taking hold at any time from the moment before our flies fall on the water to that in which we lift them for another cast. We miss, no doubt, more fish, but the quality of the surprise we court is infinitely more various. It is for that reason that I would not be debarred from Ribble, Wharfe, or Eden in exchange for the freedom of any chalk river, delightful though that fishing is in its prim, ceremonial way.

Surprise, not too long delayed, is almost essential to good fishing. A rise at your first cast, even though not followed by another, has a wonderful effect on your fishing for several hours. There are not many men who can fish all morning without seeing or feeling a fish and not suffer some deterioration in care or keenness that is likely to retard their reaction when at last the moment comes. It takes one surprise after another, repeated at not too infrequent intervals, to keep the fisherman up to the mark. On a dead day, fishing the stream, the angler, satisfied with the technique of his performance and blaming the fish or the weather for his empty basket, is startled by the sudden plunge of a half-pounder at the end of his line and only then becomes aware that he has been fishing very badly, so markedly does the surprise of that despaired-of capture tauten his nerves and improve him as a fisherman.

Surprise given by the fish to the angler is sometimes dependent on surprise given by the angler to the fish. The Ribble fish, for example, long under the tutelage of the Manchester Anglers, are accustomed to be fished for with very small flies. These flies they see so often that they may be supposed even to know them by name and to decide at once if they have been

75

tied at Horton or are base imitations imported from elsewhere. These flies, if they are in a taking mood, they will take, although they know them, out of proper gratitude for the care that is bestowed upon themselves. But yesterday they were not taking these flies. They would occasionally rise in recognition, as much as to say 'Orange Tinsel Partridge', in a splash of good Ribble water, but they would not lay hold. At least they would not lay hold for me and would scarcely come up, even quietly, as if to whisper 'Snipe and Yellow'. I caught nothing until I hunted out the fly that of all in my box least resembled those delicate little things that Ribble fish consider their due and expect to see in likely places during the season as often as half a dozen times a day. I picked on Hirst's Fancy, relic of a Hampshire stream, an enormous woolly-hackled, grey fly with large wings and a body thickly cased in silver tinsel. I threw it in and had a fish at once. Why? Because it was so unlike anything a Ribble fish ever sees that, after running rapidly through his list, he decided he had better try it. Surprise jolted him from being a bored observer of the artificial flies he had known from fryhood into being an investigator ready to sacrifice himself in the pursuit of truth. All fly-fishermen could remember dozens of such examples, even without referring to fish they have seen caught, whose suicide could be explained only as the result of complete loss of judgement due to surprise at the behaviour of a human windmill on the bank immediately above them and the splash of a mop of feathers in front of their noses. This, they might say, was what happened in my case.

Fishing in Lilliput

Not many of us can get fishing in such rivers as Test and Itchen where a pounder is a little fish. Nor can many of us fish regularly in such rivers as the Dove, the Eden and the Derby-shire Wye. We may get a day or two on such rivers in a season, but, for the most part, we have to make do with fishing less obviously good. Happily, however, the pleasure of fishing is not strictly measurable in weight of fish, or in its annual cost, and some of the most delightful days are to be had on waters where anyone may fish who has a licence, closes gates, recognizes that hedges are meant as barriers and not as sporting obstacles to be broken through, and never walks in unmown grass. These waters are of two kinds, those without any fish in them and those with many fish but small. These last, to those who know them, give some of the pleasantest fishing in the country. Sometimes, indeed, when the big rivers are out of order, many a man with the right to fish a nobler water has found himself well advised to leave that water and to go to fish in Lilliput instead.

In Lilliput everything is small, but the visiting fisherman remains, regretfully, his natural size. Small boys have an advantage in that country. Parts of the rivers in Lilliput are defended by bush and bramble which deter small boys much less than Gullivers. Other parts are so open that the man-mountain who would catch a fish there must be able to hide behind a molehill or a thistle. And, until he knows them, Gulliver is over-conscious of indignity in creeping so low to catch such little fish. For in the rivers of Lilliput the trout run small, from six to sixteen to the pound (some say thirty-two) though you will always meet a man who knew a man who hooked and lost a great fish that was six ounces if it was a drachm. In Lilliput men who elsewhere jeer at an eight-inch limit are inclined to complain of a six-inch limit as too big. Returning from Lilliput to the normal-sized world men find themselves excusing the little fish by saying that 'they eat very sweet'. So they do, but to say so is like finding that the best that can be said of a man is that 'he made a beautiful corpse'. The little fish of Lilliput deserve a handsomer obituary. Let me suggest a few of the praises that they earn. They are great fighters of their inches. There is almost no day on which they will not rise. When they rise, they rise heartily. Indeed they rise with such decision and promptitude that they ought to be both wealthy and wise. Very wise they are not. Wealthy? They are not in a rich country but in one where to keep a full stomach is riches. And they, by August, are plump as little aldermen and a great deal livelier.

The secret of getting the best out of fishing in Lilliput is to pretend that you are fishing in Brobdingnag. Attack a rising three-ounce fish as if you were trying to get a rise out of a three-pounder. It is as difficult and therefore as interesting to float your dry fly past that diminutive nose as it is to offer it to a larger fish. You will probably get more fish with your three wet flies, but you will get more satisfaction out of a single dry one. The dry fly, even when taken by one of these hop-o'-my-thumbs, requires a deliberation in the strike which gives to a rise an importance far greater than can ever be attributed to the sudden pluck and pull that make up the simultaneous rise and strike proper to the wet fly. Use a rod that will cast a short line and use the finest tackle you can get. Give yourself a chance of being broken by one of the rare quarter-pound veterans of the river. If you find you are getting too many fish, raise your size limit – by quarter inches. A careful adjustment of mind and tackle alike will give you days of as good fishing in Lilliput as ever you could get among the Brobdingnagian monsters. Disregard absolutely the advice of the books about fishing straight on if you fail to rise a fish that you have spotted. Make up your mind that if you choose to catch a particular fish of large size (say seven inches) you will catch him, if you have to smoke a pipe between each cast. Watch the fly on the water as if you were fishing for the epicures of the chalk streams. If the fish in Lilliput have a vice (which I do not like to admit), it is that they are too willing to take any fly you offer them. But even in Lilliput it will be found that on each day there is one fly that they will more willingly take than any other. If you make your own flies, you can be surer of appreciation in Lilliput than elsewhere, but here and there you will come across a little trout who rejects your fly and yet takes another the moment it has passed him. Such a trout is very valuable, no matter what his size, and when you outwit him by giving him just the fly he is preferring, he will set you up in your own mind for half a day.

My own favourite river in Lilliput is (but who gives away such secrets?) the —. It turns almost into a river of Brobdingnag before it reaches the sea, but that is many miles away. Tiny as it is, it is three rivers in one, providing three several sorts of fishing. One length of it, where the quarter-pound veterans lie, is in a deep gully, overhung with trees, almost dark at midday. Here, in the tunnel of green leaves, are short deep pools. You must wade if you are to get near the water at all and stoop if you are to get along under the boughs. There is no room for a nine-foot rod. This length is for the hottest days. Another length is fast, though much broken with Lilliput boulders. It invites the wet fly. (A greedy friend took six dozen trout from this length one day using three wet flies.) Even here a burly, bushy little dry fly is a pleasant sight dancing down the rapids and does, I think, take slightly bigger fish. The third length is the best. Its water is slow, with weeds instead of boulders. Its pools are very long, with a slowly smoothing surface below the runs. The only cover on either side of it is given by short rushes, each of which just now carries one of those little tufts which will not part with any fly that touches it. It is, in fact, a perfect length for dry fly fishing. The man who has fished up that short length and reached the top of it with, say, six fish and his temper well in hand has done something to be proud of. And, since the fish are Lilliput fish, he is not punished for his success by a heavy weight to carry as he walks back down the valley, the last of the sunlight on the mountains, the white scuts of the rabbits vanishing in the dusky fields and the first owls calling. In Lilliput no sunset is ever spoiled by the strap of a heavy basket insistently cutting the shoulder.

Saving a Blank

There is no such thing as a blank fishing day for the fisherman. It will be saved for him by the white-throated weasel, who watches his fishing from a hole in the stone wall under which is lying a fish that refused all flies; or by the excitement of identifying insects; or by the apple-blossom in a near-by orchard; and no one could call that day a blank on which he has seen a kingfisher. Other people do not understand this, and no fisherman likes to return with the empty basket which, at home, means an indubitable blank, not to be explained by reference to weather or water and not to be disproved by reference to seemingly irrelevant things, such as the spread whisks of flying duns, the tentative dipping of the spinners, or the tropic flash of the kingfisher through sunlight and shadow. An empty basket is decidedly a thing to be avoided, even if it were not for that desirable difference in everything that is noticeable when after several hours of failure a fisherman is suddenly engaged in a tussle with a fish. As the time draws to an end when, properly speaking, the fish should be engaged in their 'morning rise' to artificial flies, with the basket still empty and the rod unbent, the fisherman begins to look for remedies.

Of these there are many, though sometimes one too few. Most consist in a radical change in the way of fishing. I have written of the element of surprise. A little of that will sometimes save a blank. That is the excuse for the splashing of a monstrous Hirst's Fancy before fish habitually flattered by being offered none but delicate Yorkshire flies. In the same way, where fish are accustomed to take flies of a fair size, a blank may sometimes be saved by offering them midgets, when fish which have taken to straining at camels will swallow a gnat, such a little one, but still to their surprise big enough to hold a hook. Another good dodge for evading blanks is to desert the 'smittal' places, always over-fished, and to offer a dry fly to a fish in a place where it has come to think itself impregnable. This, of course, is to be done by the wet-fly fisherman on water usually fished with wet flies. On such water I have seen a fish come up to look at a floating fly, turn from it, and, as it slowly drifted down, visibly have a second thought and come at it again, this time in earnest, giving in a second or two as much excitement as a whole basketful of fish that took hold under water. The reasoning of that fish was, no doubt, 'This looks like an artificial fly, and today we are not taking any.' His second thought was: 'But all artificial flies are sunk. This thing floats. Have at it. . . .' Oddly enough, the dry-fly fisherman, if he be no purist committed to the stoic acceptance of blank days, turns in last resort to the wet fly and dips it in glycerine to make it sink. With these chalk-stream fish of his, boasted untakable unless with a fly perfectly cast and perfectly floating, he reverts to the most primitive but one of all forms of fly-fishing, and tries them with a sunk fly, sometimes even fishing it downstream, though he looks round guiltily to see that no one is watching him. Sir Herbert Maxwell, writing of such a day, describes aloofly, as one writing of sacrilege, the capture of a chalk-stream trout with a big sunk Palmer with two hooks.

There are certain flies which have earned a special reputation as savers of blanks. The greatest of these, in the south, is Tup:

> 'With paunch of strawberry and cream,
>   Dun hackle, primrose tail,
> A Tup, fished wet or made to swim,
>   But never known to fail. . . .'

Never? There are days when even Tup is rejected. The gold-ribbed Hare's Ear has its adherents. Many entrust their last hopes to a Wickham. To this list I am inclined to add Hardy's Pale Watery Nymph. Henceforth it has, until ousted by a better, its place in that waistcoat pocket first-aid outfit for blank days, the little box that holds these occasional conjurers. But there is another fly for which I would, if necessary, sacrifice any of these. It owes its virtue as a blank-saver less to anything odd or unusual than to the character of the days on which it is most efficacious. These are days of brilliant sunshine, windless or almost windless, when the water is under a haze of small dark insects, and the trout, rejecting solid dishes like the duns, suck down nothing but these minute savouries. These days have a decided tendency towards blankness, and if proof of this were needed it is to be found in the dissatisfaction with which fisherman have regarded one after another imitation of the black gnat. Ronald's Black Gnat had a body of black ostrich herl and dark starling wings. Francis's dressing was black ostrich herl, very small, black hackle, and 'two very fine clear strips of starlings feather, dressed as low and flat as you can conveniently fix them.' He says, pertinently, that when this fly is on the water the fish will seldom take the imitation, or indeed any other artificial. Pike scales have been used for its wings, and it has been made wingless of badger hackle. Halford improved on all these, but though he said 'the fly is scarcely black and certainly is not a gnat,' tradition was too strong even for him. It was left to Mr Dunne to discover that so far from being black it is all the colours of the rainbow, iridescent, in fact. His fly, with honey hackle and for wings a bunch of bottle-green and fiery red fibres, is a notable blank-saver. Fish will rise to the sunshine through those red and bottle-green fibres when they will rise to nothing else.

More desperate remedies are those of a better friend than fisherman who was known to depart towards the end of a blank day to a bridge over a wooded part of the river and to return with a trout, obtained by dapping with a Coch-y-bondhu. Beetles in their natural state have saved some blanks, and so have worms, but of these deeds it is kinder not to speak.

Carelessness

With the morning gone, and with it the best of the 'taking time', and the river thin and unpromising, I went up to have a look at the tarn on the hillside, and in the afternoon and evening got five fish, of which only two were worthy of the place. That is one of the blemishes of still-water fishing. The feeding fish cruise for their dinners instead of taking places and having their dinners served to them by an obsequious stream. In the stream they are as strict upon the point of precedence as diplomatists' wives at a reception, so that a fisherman who knows his business knows where is the head of the table, where the most coveted seats, and, since precedence among fish is an affair of strength, finds it possible to offer his flies to the better fish. In the lake it is very nearly a matter of luck whether you get big fish or little ones. All you can do is to fish as well as you know how, to hope for the luck of putting your fly rightly in the close neighbourhood of a big fish who may feel disposed to take it, to see a rise and then another, and to be right, instead of wrong, in your assumption that both rises are made by the same fish and in your consequent deduction of the direction in which he is moving. The chance nature of tarn-fishing is derogatory to human dignity – like betting on horses you have never seen, or marriage in those countries where women are invisible until they are wed.

You can, however, get something from it, as from all fishing. On Monday I got the knock-down blow of a lesson against carelessness. For a very long time I have been hoping to get one of the really big trout that certainly lurk in that place. An unworthy hope, like the hope to win the big prize in a lottery. I had tried to make it less unworthy by tying one or two flies with which to delude myself into the belief that I had contributed something to the luck that should bring him at last to try conclusions with my rod. I never thought of him in the net or on land, but often in imagination I had felt the deep 'cello thrumming of the big fellow down in the dark water by the end of the broken wall. Perhaps there was carelessness in not imagining a little more. For I did indeed get exactly what I had imagined, but no more. That fish is still in the tarn. Now, the special flies I had tied for him were a Golden Tippet with silver body for a bright day and an improved version of Teal and Green. I cannot remember who it was who, when looking through my box of lake and sea-trout flies, told me that apple-green wool is better for the body of this fly than the poisonous, violent green to be seen on all bought specimens. But, thinking of the grandfather of the tarn, I tied me a Teal and Applegreen and was very well pleased with its look in the water. I also got three fish on it, and none on the ordinary Teal and Green, which I fished on the same cast. But I did not get the grand-father. When the superior virtue of Apple-green had been proved, I removed the ordinary Teal and Green from its position as tail fly, thinking to put Apple-green in its place. But Apple-green was on a very short length of gut as middle dropper, and if I were to take it off the gut would be shorter still. So I thought I would give the Butcher a chance and put him on at the tail, leaving well alone with Apple-green. There was plenty of time for this sort of shilly-shallying, for there was no wind on the tarn, and for long intervals not enough even to drift a boat across the smooth water. Just as I had the Butcher fixed, however, the water was ruffled by a slight breeze some twenty yards from where I was. I was in a hurry to get there, and, somehow, the Butcher caught in one of the rowlocks. I jerked it free and a moment later was at the top of the rippled water. I saw a small quiet rise, and cast towards it, letting the flies rest. It was a longish cast, and some line lay on the water. The line suddenly became alive, I struck, and down went a really heavy fish. There was no mistaking that plunging weight. Deep down, he swam in towards the boat, while I reeled in like mad. Then, suddenly, he shook his head, rushed to the surface, showed me a great side and head, and was gone. I reeled in and looked at the Butcher. The point and barb of the hook had gone when I caught it in the rowlock. I was well paid for my carelessness. The fisherman always is. The rusted hook in the spinner put away damp loses his biggest pike, the line undried after a day's fishing breaks and loses him his best tackle, the reel unoiled jams at the moment when the carp is making its most tremendous rush, the gaff unlooked to twists in the socket of the handle and loses the salmon of the year. But the easiest piece of carelessness of all, and the swiftest rewarded, is disregard of the points of your fly-hooks. And the enormity of the punishment seems the greater when we think of the seeming slightness of the thing we have neglected, a faint click behind our backs when casting from a stony bank, even the act of unhooking a fish, and in this case an incident that would never have been remembered except for its tremendous consequences.

Fishing Inns

Fishing inns are of two kinds, good ones and downright swindles. As the holiday months draw to an end, most fishermen have something to say about one or other. It is noticeable that they say a good deal more about the downright swindles than about inns of the other kind. This is not because there are more of them, but because a good fishing inn is something that is not often given away. The man who has found such an inn is inclined to keep it to himself, lest by becoming too well known it should come to hold more visitors than there are fish in its waters, and so deteriorate into one of the downright swindles. These everybody knows. Their advertisements are shameless anachronisms, since they describe as good fishing the depleted waters that were well enough fifty years ago. For them the fishing is merely what the feathers are to the bare hook, a means to attract, but a travesty of what is promised. The visitors to these places are always new to the water, for no man would ever go there twice. The new-comer finds himself among other new-comers, bamboozled like himself, and, like them, hearing from the landlord of the great catches that have been made there in some golden age, lingers from day to day until his holiday is gone and he is himself almost out of conceit with the sport that has filled his dreams for months before. There is no one to undeceive him. All are new and full of hope, and do not realize until it is too late that the only successful angling in that place is done by the landlord, and that they are themselves the poor fish who rose to a lie in an advertisement, were played and landed, and will at last be 'put back', wise enough at least not to rise to that particular advertisement again. That is, indeed, their only revenge, for they have been fed and bedded, and if they have paid an extravagant price for board and lodging on account of the fish which, not being in the river, are not to be caught, no one to whom they complain will understand their bitterness or put down their empty baskets to anything but their inadequate skill. It will be a long time before the *Anglers' Diary*, for example, that invaluable guide to fishing, good and bad alike, has the courage to copy Baedeker and to distribute stars to those hotels where the fishing is really good and whole constellations to those whose fishing deserves it. When that day comes we shall judge fishermen with more accurate regard to the waters in which they fish, and the man who gets his brace of half-pounders from the waters of a fishing inn with one star will hold up his head with the man who has got his dozen brace from the ten-starred water elsewhere. Meanwhile there is nothing to be done, except to demand some more accurate description of the fishing than the word 'good', which, in the interests of an inn-keeper, is sometimes applied to the barrenest waters in the kingdom.

Good fishing inns are easily defined. They are inns the guests of which have the opportunity of good fishing. If they give us that, we can forgive them all else. Their beds may be boards, their food uneatable except at the close of a good day, when a fisherman will swallow anything. One of the best I ever knew was not an inn at all, but a peasant's barn, inhabited by rats and chickens and such an enormous quantity of fleas that the sleepiest of men could count on being on the water at sunrise. The food was black bread and the fish we caught, with plenty of eggs and plenty of milk. We washed in the river, for there was nowhere else for that purpose. To get to that place we drove for thirty miles along a bad road and nearly as many where there was no road at all, but we drove with delight, laughing at the bumps which on any other journey would have been no laughing matter, for we were going to the river or coming back from it, and on that river we counted it a poor day if we had not our ten brace of trout and grayling apiece. Perhaps that old barn, on the cliff above the river, is no fair example. But there are plenty of such places in England. If the fishing is good, nothing else matters much. If I were writing a guide to fishing lodgings and fishing inns I should give that barn five stars, whereas I should give no star at all to the famous — at —, where the beds would satisfy the princess in the fairy tale and they serve a six-course dinner at night and a five-course luncheon in the middle of day. Luncheon in the middle of the day betrays a bad fishing inn (unless on one of those sea-trout rivers that are fished at night). In a good fishing inn they have forgotten how to make luncheons, for all their guests grab sandwiches, rush out immediately after breakfast and come back hungry for dinner with the sandwiches still in their pockets, because they have never had time to eat them. An inn that expects its guests to come in for luncheon in the middle of the day is an inn with a bad conscience, which knows that its water is not worth fishing.

It is best, of course, if the people of the inn are a little interested in fishing. They should know enough to say the right things. I do not much like it if the landlord himself fishes. If he fishes too well he is apt to be a bore. If he fishes too badly he is apt to be a butt. We can do well without either. The widow of a fisherman makes a good hostess for a fishing inn. Her relationship to actual fishing is near enough but not too near. She will not think that it is a good fishing day because the rain is coming down, and she will have learnt not only to accept excuses for failure but even to feel when they are necessary and to offer them herself. A good fishing inn is enhanced by a picture or two by Rolfe or some stuffed fish, but these should have the dates and places of their capture clearly visible inside the cases. There are bad fishing inns, I have been told, that buy stuffed fish and hang them in their halls as a sort of ground bait. Lastly, of course, a good fishing inn has the right visitors. These are simple, kindly fellows, not desperate 'eye-wipers' of the kind so delicately described by William Caine. They may disagree on all subjects but one. That one is a rhyme known as the Fisherman's Prayer. On that they should be unanimous. If any mutton-headed purveyor of second-hand wit should so much as begin to lead up to the quotation of that rhyme, they should be the sort of men who, without a word said, would arise all together and take that man and drown him in the river.

The Local Angler and the Others

A correspondent, in sending me a report on his river, remarks, 'River too low for good fishing. Local fishermen have been making big catches.' The distinction drawn is most just. 'Good fishing' is an unprofitable business. It is the fishing of the visiting angler. Local fishing, on the other hand, is doing quite nicely, but then it is of a very different kind. In the early months of the season, the distinction is not so marked. The visitor does as well as the local, but now, when the yellow flag irises are blazing by the river where it runs through the lowland meadows, when the big stones that once made a fine shelter for a trout when the water swept over the top of them are standing high with a ragged fringe of dried moss, when hay-making has begun and cut grass comes drifting down, the conditions for 'good fishing' are poor. Anglers are now divided into local fishermen and those others who toil for nothing through the heat of the day and go home to their evening meals when the local men are thinking of putting their rods together. The local angler is always inclined to look with pity on the visitor, but when days grow hot and the sea-trout begin to run, his pity becomes tinged with scorn.

Sea-trout are running in plenty up one well-known river, but only an odd one or two have been caught. I asked a local angler why. 'Well,' said he, 'they come from the towns and they hurry down to the river and can't wait till dusk but throw their flies in right away, and by the time they ought to begin they have frightened every fish in the pool. When they have had a fair lot of blanks they stop coming and then it's time enough for us to start.' It is the same thing with the brown trout. The local angler, in this weather, does not go down to the river till just before sunset. If he does fish the river by day, he passes by all the places where trout would be taking in other circumstances and goes straight to the places where there is a chance of getting one now. But, mostly, if he takes a day's fishing, he leaves the river alone. He watches the visitor wading the main stream, his handsome rod flashing merrily in the powerful sunlight. He says nothing. He has had the best of the season's fly-fishing in the river and now is turning to the becks and minor tributaries which, happily for him, the visitor disregards altogether. He will apply the same methods in the main river if there are not too many people trying to do 'good fishing' there. He carries an old dull rod with which he can cast a fly if opportunity offers, but stiff enough for a more profitable business. He fishes mostly neither dry fly nor sunk fly, but uses instead the old wet worm and creeps up the little stream like an Indian, throwing his Stewart or Pennell tackle (or single small hook which is better than the big one of our ancestors) before him into the places in which he caught fish last year and the year before, and the year before that, the places in which, if he were a trout, he would choose to lie Sympathetic, intimate imagination combined with experience is the whole secret of successful worm-fishing. There, under that willow, the bank curves; there, just ahead of that little pillow in the water, must be a pocket big enough for a trout; there under that overhanging tussock must be a cool lie; a good trout is always to be found in this gully, where the little water of the stream is given depth in exchange for breadth; at the corner of that stone is the taking place. The worm swings forward and dives without a splash, the line suddenly quivers and a moment later a fat quarter-pounder is on his way to join his cousins in the basket. And so up the stream. At the mill-dam, if a bit of breeze is rippling the surface, the local fisher winds his worm cast round his hat and puts on instead a cast of flies. The mill-dam is sometimes good for a brace or two. Then, off with the flies and on with the worm again, sinking it for a moment just above the lip of the dam where there is always the chance of a big one. After that up the narrowing beck, now wading ankle deep between close trees, now wriggling through the bushes on the banks, sometimes, with a good fish, wishing he had a landing net, sometimes, when in a thicket of brambles, thanking his stars that he has not, and so up out of the valley to the high moorland where curlews scream overhead and lapwings noisily mistake the fisherman for an enemy. The young peewits are about just now, and might be mistaken for chickens newly hatched if it were not that as soon as they begin to run about they imitate so exactly the characteristic pose of the older birds. At last, high above the valley, with his basket brimming, the local fisherman rests on the heather and looks below him. The little beck that has given him his sport is nowhere to be seen, but far down in the lowland, a broad ribbon of silver shining in the sun, the famous river is dotted here and there with the figures of those who have come from far away to seek 'good fishing' and with the river at this height on this day might almost as well be laying their flies upon a looking-glass.

Dourness

'All in a hot and copper sky
The bloody Sun, at noon . . .'

COLERIDGE.

There was the appearance of a fair water, but the trout seemed to be different fish from those which came so willingly to the fly before the heat-wave reached us. On such days as these, the fisherman who picks up his brace of fish before night is happy and feels he has wrested something from implacable fate. If his trout are to be of any size, he seeks them with the floating fly and to find a fish willing to take that fly he has to walk and cast and cast and walk again until his arm aches and his back feels as if he had been carrying coals. His faculty of faith has been as severely exercised as his muscles. In fishing the wet fly, that faculty is less required. After all, the wet fly is on the other side of that glittering mirror of water. It is 'through the looking-glass', where it is easy to believe that anything may happen at any time. At least the wet fly is on the same side of the looking-glass as is the fish. It seems not improbable, but even likely, that some trout or other shall see it and not the glitter of the gut. But with the dry fly it is different. It and the angler are on the same side of the looking-glass. The trout may be on the other side, but the only signs of them seen by the fisherman are given by those monstrous spoil-sports who rush out from the shallows with a great wave so far ahead of him as to make him despair of ever getting within casting range of a trout, since these have seen him at such a distance. It is only the true believer who can go on laying his fly on the water, picking it off and laying it on again as carefully as if he were presenting it to a fish whose visible rises show that he is waiting for something of the sort. The fly boats on a seemingly dead and impenetrable mirror and faith is hard put to it to keep on trusting

94

that a trout shall suddenly smash the mirror with his nose and take it under.

On such hot, glaring days, it is usual to explain failure by saying that the days or the trout are dour. There is a tremendous hatch of fly. But, instead of the hatch being the signal for eager noses to dimple the river, for the trout to form up in queues along the bank against which the flies are blown, when the happy angler can take one after another, moving slowly up the line of feeding fish, the flies seem to have been granted a general amnesty, except by the birds. They hatch. They try their wings. They flutter and drift across the water. They rise and fly away and though we know very well that the river is full of fish, not a fly has his flutterings ended in a splash. If, on such days, the dry fly fisherman were to wait until he could follow the example of the south countrymen, the doctors of Itchen and Test, who first, with butterfly net or binoculars, ascertain what fly the fish are taking, differentiating even between the sexes, and put on accordingly Pale Watery (male) or BWO (female), he would wait until the end of the day with never a fly on his cast, for the simple reason that since no fish are feeding on visible flies, if he puts on a copy of one of the flies that he sees he can expect only that it will share its neglect by the trout. There is no hope in putting on a fly exactly like the real ones. The fisherman must put on a fly that is somehow more attractive than they. Since he cannot tell what that may be, he has a wide choice. My own rule on such days is to put on a fly that suits me (because I can easily see it) and to trust that it will suit the trout. Ginger Quill is pleasantly visible. So is a good big Wickham. So is one of Hardy's Pale Olives dressed 'Refracta' fashion. To the fisherman it looks on the water like a bundle of pale fluff and its long hackles disturb the surface in a way to make a trout look at it, even against his will. It pays, in this business of continual casting without the invitation of a rise, to change the fly often. Each change renews the angler, even if it does not affect the fish.

And on dour days, so called, the angler needs a lot of re-newing. A few hours without response abbreviate his temper and leave him altogether unfit to maintain the cheerful spirit without which fishing is a degrading pursuit. The best (that is to say, the keenest) fishermen fare worst. The dilettantes give up early and gather at the inn to discuss the weather. The brace or brace and a half that is all that rewards the man who will not be beaten by the weather is like the scholar's guerdon, scarcely to be appreciated by the world at large. They look so little and have cost so much. For on dour days the lightness of the basket is made up for by a great weight of all manner of afflictions. It is on a dour day that the fisherman loses his landing net and does not discover his loss until he is playing his second, last and best fish in a difficult place. It is on a dour day that he finds a score of bare-footed children paddling all over the long broken stretch to which he had been looking to retrieve his failure; that the lads of the village are bathing in his favourite pool; that though, during the last two months, he has acquired some confidence in himself, he finds that he is casting as badly as ever he was; that to fish against the sun he must also fish against the wind; that though his flies will not catch fish they will catch everything else within reach; that 4x gut will not stand an impatient tug when the Wickham has risen and hooked a willow tree; that local anglers insist on telling him how, during the last spate, when the water was thick, they caught twenty fish in an hour on worm, or how they suppose he is fishing 'just for sport'; that in this heat it is as easy to get wet in waders as without them; that after fishing up two miles of river it is a six-mile walk to get back. I observe that during haymaking in this weather, the farmers, while very cheerful, use continuous horrible language to their horses. It has occurred to me that fisherman might preserve their happy calm by keeping up a similar harangue to the trout. It would not affect the fish, but it might relieve the fishermen. For I come to think that when we say the fish are dour we are attributing to them the effect they produce in ourselves. When we call the fish dour, they are probably in the best of spirits, having eaten their fill during the last flood, or taking it easy through the heat of the day, lying quietly in the water, while the angler toils in the hot air, and looking forward to a handsome feast in the cool after sundown, when the angler, tired completely out, is on his way home, telling himself that he has had plenty of fresh air and looking forward to tomorrow's work as to a restful holiday.

Bulls and Kindred Phenomena

The trout-fisher's is one of the more dangerous sports. Cricketers and Golfers play as it were in glass cases. The worst dangers of the countryside are fenced off from them. They are like the bathers at Singapore, who swim inside a palisade that keeps out the sharks. The solitary trout-fisher, on the other hand, can never be sure that he will not in the twinkling of an eye be transformed from the hunter to the hunted. Of course there are good bulls, but who shall know whether a bull be good or bad without inviting so close an acquaintanceship that it cannot be remedied if the bull turns out not to be good. Men of weak nerves take a whole year in which to recover after a fortnight's fishing holiday in a dairy farming country. One such I know who extends his dread to cows as well as bulls. He can never feel sure, he says, that they do not take after the male side of the family. I do not go so far as that. I am hail-fellow-well-met with any cow that does not splash among the rising fish. But, when there is a bull about, I have no sort of doubt as to which is the better side of the river. Sometimes, even to be on the better side of the river is an insufficient precaution. It is an altogether insufficient precaution in the presence of a bull who is definitely interested in the difference between wet and dry flies. I have recently met such a bull. Inspirited by rain, the trout had begun to rise as they often do just before the becks begin to colour the river. I had done nothing earlier in the afternoon and knew that I must make the most of the rise while it lasted. Heavy rain far up the valley promised a spate. I had got a brace of half-pounders on Waterhen and Yellow and was casting to a third, who was rising in a little eddy on the far side of the river, when this bull became suddenly an important feature of the landscape. He came to the bank opposite me and looked down into the eddy, young, powerful, impatient and, as it appeared, inquisitive. I failed to get that fish and moved up. I got another fish on the Waterhen when the bull observed in a decidedly truculent voice that my proceedings displeased him. I did not care, because I was on the better side of the river. I got a fish on the Blue Hawk. The bull tried to toss a clump of grass. Just then, looking back, I saw the trout in the eddy rise again. He had refused my wet flies, so I changed my cast for a tapered one with a fluffy grey fly on the end of it. The changing of casts interested the bull exceedingly. He followed when I worked down the river again until I was in a position to cast across to the eddy. The first cast was a failure, dropping below the trout. At the second up he came, down went my fly and a few minutes later I was putting the best fish of the day into the creel. The bull was beside himself with interest in this change of technique. He came lumbering down the bank into the water and finding it deep went up river along his own side. By this time there was a good deal of water in the river and it had begun to colour. I had hardly replaced my wet flies before I perceived that I was no longer on the better side of the river. That bull, wishing to know the difference between wet and dry flies, had swum the river higher up and was approaching me grimly, inevitably, like a thunder-cloud, along my own bank. There are those who in such circumstances advise presence of mind in the form of an impenetrable calm, which, they say, will disarm the most ferocious of bulls. For my part I think that sort of presence of mind is best which most rapidly produces absence of body. I retired. The bull followed. I cut a corner. The bull foresaw that manoeuvre and did the same. I quickened, slightly, my pace. So did he. A split cane of Hardy's is an excellent weapon, but not for all purposes. That beast crossed three stone walls and lost interest only at the fourth. And there are those who say that fishing is the re-creation of the contemplative man.

Kindred phenomena to bulls are wasps, mosquitoes and clegs. In the character of his attack, the wasp is like the bull. He is noisy and his presence rasps the nerves. His ultimate thrust is not so dangerous, but the spectacle of him buzzing round deciding when to make it does not help the neat delivery of a cast of flies. Unlike the bull, he is worst when in the bosom of his family. Wasps' nests ripen at the season of the year when good fish have to be stalked. With his eye on the place where a trout rose, the fisherman creeps and sidles along the bank. He would willingly leave that trout alone rather than put hand or foot in the wasps' nest or even brush its threshold with his coat. But the wasps make no allowances and pour out to the attack as if he had offended them on purpose. Wasp grubs are much used by the roach-fishers. From the trout-fisher's point of view, the more they use the better. Mosquitoes are not so bad. They are like the indigestion that follows indulgence in gingerbreads, but does not spoil the gingerbread's delightful taste. It is only when fishing is not good that we notice them. When it is good we notice only the subsequent painful lumps. In England, that is. Abroad I have known them so numerous and poisonous that fishing was like the old Christmas game of snapdragon. Worst of these minor horrors are clegs. Their bites are not so painful as the wasp's sting. But, on the other hand, the wasp seldom does sting. The horror with the wasp is in expectancy. The horror with the cleg is that he bites without warning. His flight is noiseless. He settles as lightly as I would wish my fly to settle on the stream. There follows a moment of sharp pain, when the fisherman smites his cheek or wrist and slays a brownish, big-headed, blood-swollen beast. That is but the beginning of his agony. He sees the next and smites before it bites. The third beats him again. The fourth and fifth settle on his sleeve in error. As he brushes them off, the sixth gets its sucker home in his forehead. Thereafter, at midday, he is like a man fighting a legion of fiends in the dark. Clegs, wasps and mosquitoes, however, shall never keep me from the river during a good rise. Bulls are different. As a trout-fisher, I prefer to be alone. But a bull puts me out of love with solitude and I envy the gregarious, regimented roach-fishers. Their multitude is their strength. The most truculent of bulls will hardly face an array of fifty men, even if their floats are red.

Making Spinning Interesting

When the late Mr Illingworth was engaged in inventing his much-abused and often misused reel, he had in view the desirability of being able to cast a minnow a long way without having to handicap it as a bait by fixing a lead in front of it to act like the man with the red flag who used to parade solemnly in front of the steam-roller. It probably had not occurred to him that he would, by doing this, end by changing altogether the fisherman's conception of what is and what is not 'a good minnowing water'. Yet that is what the new perfection of light spinning tackle has brought about. Of course, others beside Mr Illingworth were at work improving spinning reels, just as there were a host of men engaged in hurrying the evolution of the steam-roller into the motor-car. In considering the new character of spinning what has to be said applies not to the Illingworth reel alone, but to the latest and best American 'level-winding, free-wheel, multipliers' and to half a dozen fixed spool reels used with fine lines. The essential point about all these reels is that it is possible with them to cast with great accuracy a comparatively light bait. It is usually assumed that their sole virtue lies in the distance to which such a bait can be cast. But distance is only occasionally an object. There is seldom need for the long casts which, under the old system, could easily be made with a heavily weighted bait. The real advantage lies not so much in the distance from the angler at which the bait begins to swim, as in the shallowness of the water in which, thanks to its lightness, it is possible to swim it.

Distance is attainable, no doubt, and is, at first, seductive. But concentration on it leads rapidly to complete loss of interest in spinning. After the first discovery that it is possible to rise and hook a trout so far away that you have difficulty in believing that you and he are in any way related to each other, you very soon come to discover that, if you persist in long casting, you are exchanging fishing for fish. Catching fish is so easy by this method that there is no pleasure in it whatsoever. That is to say, of course, catching fish on the days on which twenty years ago one would have said there was a good water for spinning. In such water any energetic donkey casting long distances across the river will find that, without the slightest exercise of observation or of skill beyond that of the mechanical manipulation of his reel, he has plenty of fish in his basket. Spinning becomes interesting again only when we apply the new technique not to the task that was within the reach of the old but to a task that was altogether beyond it. The water that is right for the new as opposed to the old spinning is not the copper-coloured water after a flood, is not the full river, but the river when it is generally given up as a bad job, very low, very clear, when fish and (or) fishermen are at their dourest. It is a safe rule to spin only on those days when you can be almost sure that not a fly-fisherman will be on the river. Then and then only there is some interest in spinning besides the sport to be obtained by the man who feels that he deserves some small revenge on the fish for their indifference even to a floating Wickham. It is suggested that dourness is due to some change in the chemical composition of the water. But the very dourest of fish will open his mouth and obey 'the absolute shall' of a minnow that is put before him in the right way.

After a day of spinning in these conditions I have been met more than once with the words 'I suppose you got them in the pools,' from fishermen who knew how very little water there was anywhere else. But curiously enough it is not in the pools that one gets them, at least during the brighter part of the day, which is proper to this kind of fishing. The river is too low for long casting up into a pool from below, because water too shallow to bear the minnow (that is, less than six inches of water), lies between the fisherman and the low end of any pool. The fisherman casting up into a pool cannot help being near enough to be seen by the trout in the low end of it when (as may be seen by as many as half a dozen converging waves) they turn down-stream after the minnow. If he does not get a fish with his first cast up into a pool from the run below, those fish that have seen him will go up into the body of the pool spreading the news and make it unlikely that he will get one anywhere else. It is usually better to leave the pool alone and, after carefully stalking, to concentrate on one cast up into the neck of it. Of course, if a pool is broken by rocks, destroying under these conditions its poolish nature, something may be done by regarding each rock as the back of an arm-chair against which an idle trout may be leaning and throwing up past the rock as if to jog the trout's elbow. Among these idle loungers you may well find one who is eager and willing, though you are more likely to find one in the neck. But the general plan of campaign does not put pools in the first or even in the second place. It is based on what knowledge of the river the fisherman has acquired and the translation of that knowledge into terms of very low water. For example, the fisherman remembers a hole that once surprised him in a flattish stretch. The main stretch has today run down almost to nothing, but that old hole will be a sort of oyster-shell, a saucer let into the river bed, in the hollow of which a fat trout will surely be lying. You must spin your minnow in six inches of water so that it just crosses the edge of the saucer on the side farthest from the sun. It will be great odds that you will see a swirl like a question mark straightening out as the trout turns and dashes over the edge after your disappearing minnow. Then, with low water, branches that usually trail in the river or hang so as to make an impenetrable curtain, will be high enough above the surface to let you shoot your minnow under them. There is nearly always a hole by the roots of a tree and, if all goes well, the inhabiting trout will not ask where your minnow comes from before he grabs him.

Then, too, there are the trout taking sun-baths. These are the hardest of any, for they lie in very shallow water, unfishable unless you have acquired the trick of getting your minnow to start on its way home before it touches the water at all. In these shallows, close along the edge, the minnows swarm and sometimes you may see a trout swirling among them and the minnows fretting the surface like hail in simultaneous effort to escape. That trout is yours, if excitement does not make you bungle. In such water you will have to spin your minnow so near the surface that it will make a wave and it is not easy to control your own excitement when you see the minnow's tiny wave followed close by the wave of a trout, sometimes almost to your feet before the two coalesce and your rod nearly jerks your fingers from the reel handle. On such a day you will not get the basket that is yours for the asking in a full water, but you will have earned what you get and it is just that that distinguishes fishing from the mere collection of fish.

The Winged Ant

I did not go to the Ant. The Ant came to me. He came not alone but in a crowd. A dozen or so of him (the winged red ant) were crawling in my happily disused fireplace. More were on the bookshelves, on the table, on the floor. After ungratefully spending some time in trying to get rid of them, it occurred to me that they could only have come for one purpose. They were, so to speak, artists' models clamouring for a sitting. So I put one in a small glass test-tube and set up the flymaker's vice. Then, as one interested in the history of the art, I looked up the Old Masters and compared their dressings of the Winged Ant with this invader.

The Red as well as the Black Winged Ant has been well known to fishermen as one of those flies which on certain days are good to fill a basket. The Winged Ant's is a shortish season, like that of strawberries and cream. It is at its height in August, when, particularly in woodland streams, the insect finds its way to the water in great quantities when the trout become quickly aware of its nourishing qualities, acquire, perhaps, a liking for the taste of formic acid and gulp it down in preference to anything else. It was known as an artificial fly before the middle of the eighteenth century. A hundred years later, Ronalds (1836) gives a dressing; peacock herl tied with red-brown silk, starling wing, and red hackle. Pulman (1841) remarked that he did not care much about it but gave a dressing; copper-colour peacock herl, red hackle, dark red silk and jay wing. He observed that the wings should lie flat along the body. Theakston (1853) speaks of it with more respect and gives a dressing for it among his flies for June, though his notes on the specimens he observed are under dates in August and

September. Of August he says: 'The ants sometimes fall numerous on the waters this month and are greedily taken by the fish'. 'Bright amber' with 'thin glassy wings', 'Body and legs red brown'. 'Took one off a spider's web at Robin Hood, which sparkled in the sun with fire and gold, and of a dull amber transparency.' He speaks of the dark red of head, thorax and body. 'Are altogether glassy and smooth, but a fine short hair may be seen, through a glass, on the parts which in the sun throw off short gilded reflections.' 'They are well taken by the fishes whenever they come on the water.' Theakston's dressing is: peacock body, red or amber tying silk, a few fibres of red brown mohair worked in for legs and wings from snipe or starling.

In this dressing (for a wet fly) peacock is the remarkable ingredient, though even the ruddiest bronze herl can hardly give the luminous chestnut or the apparent hardness of the actual insect. Francis (1867) and Pritt (1885) use the same material, though Pritt hackles his fly with a feather from the Blue Tit's tail. 'It will now and then do great execution, particularly after a flight of ants.' In 1916 Edmonds and Lee, the authors of *Brook and River Trouting*, are sticking to the peacock, though they disregard the red legs and suggest the wings with blue hen's hackle. These are all wet flies. When we come to dry flies, we at least break away from the peacock, though Leonard West gives it as an alternative dressing. No. 28 of Halford's new series is the Brown Ant. 'Wings, pale starling. Hackle: two furnace cock hackles. The body is ingeniously made from stripped and unstripped condor quill dyed dark maroon, the unstripped being used for 'the knob at the tail end'. The result is too thickly hackled to be very like an ant, though it has caught a great many fish. Halford says it is a good grayling fly. West's dressing is much more like the insect. He copies its body in cinnamon quill, gives it 'iridescent' legs, hackle points for wings and finishes it off with mallard horns. He calls it, optimistically, 'a capital fly at all times'.

Finally, J. W. Dunne produced a Red Ant which is a great improvement on all the others, dressed with artificial silk on a white painted hook, with hackle point wings laid flat, and a dark honey hackle.

Such is the history of the Winged Ant in the hands of the fly-tyers. Dunne's dressing is so good that it is not likely to be superseded. It is, however, elaborate. White painted hooks are not always at hand and artificial silk is not the easiest stuff to work. I amused myself, with the model before me, in trying to make a likeness of it which would catch fish and could be tied by anybody in a minute or two. Now the chief impression made by the ant on the human eye (and, one must suppose, on the trout's) is that of shape, a pear-shaped body, divided by a very thin waist from the thorax, which is divided by a very thin neck from the head. Colour, I think, must come second. Now it is not difficult by using ordinary orange tying silk for the thorax and ordinary orange floss silk for the pear-shaped body on an ordinary bronzed hook to copy almost exactly both shape and colour. The floss silk seems extravagantly bright when dry, but when oiled (that is to say in the condition in which it will be fished) it darkens, like the tying silk, to a deep ruddy chestnut. In the actual insect the wings lie flat over the tail and project a little beyond it. This impression can be reproduced by tying in on the thorax a pair of hackle points. The tips of the hackles are constricted in tying in and the effect is that of narrow glassy wings. I used the palest honey hackles I could find. A few turns of red hackle supply legs and floating power. The body is more easily shaped if the floss silk is split, so as to have a narrow band to wind and so one that will not so readily become unmanageable. The total effect is not so much a Frith as a Whistler portrait of the Winged Ant, impressionist rather than realist, but to the human eye at least recognizable.

With half a dozen of these impressionist ants duly oiled in a match-box, on a hot August day, with fair water in the river, it was, of course, impossible not to hurry off to show them to the trout. On the eddy below the stone bridge was an ant. On the bridge there were more. On a flat pool in the wood just above the trout were steadily rising at something I could not see. Was it ants? It presently was. My impressionist ant had hardly floated six inches before a trout had him. Twelve fat little trout (a whole jury) mistakenly declared themselves satisfied of the innocence of my impressionist ant, besides one or two that I missed or lost. Their verdict is enough to justify me in offering this extremely simple dressing to those who one day or other are likely to need an ant or two in a hurry. With it should be the warning that on a dull day shortly afterwards, the fish would not look at the ants, but came well to other flies. The Winged Ant is not a general utility fly, but when it is good it is very good. That is when and only when the ants are on the river. That may happen any day at this time of year (August), but is likeliest to happen on a bright hot day. It has been suggested that they are attracted by the glitter of the water.

A Mixed Bag

One occasionally gets a mixed bag, fly-fishing. It may be a sea-trout among the brown, or a grilse; it may be something much less welcome. I remember an autumn day in a river in Latvia when grayling were taking the wet fly as if they had been waiting for it, and I found to my own surprise ten good dace among my grayling. In the frenzy of making the best use of a really phenomenal 'taking time', I had actually not noticed that I was catching anything but grayling. In float-fishing a man, without moving from his chosen place, may get bream, roach, perch, pike and what not. And in spinning in waters not preserved rigorously for trout, mixed bags are almost the rule. Chub where there are any take the minnow in that decisive unhurried way of theirs as if they thought it was one of their own just escaped from some domestic pen. Perch often take it close to the angler when the following trout has at last decided that he had better leave it alone. People talk of a pike 'knocking'. The rat-a-tat-tat of a perch is as unmistakable as the postman's. Pike are always possible and, hooked on trout tackle, soon shake to pieces any mistaken belief that they are dull fellows to fight. One bag this year, for an hour's fishing after tea, was a one-pound trout, a quarter-pound perch and two jack of $5\frac{3}{4}$ and 3 pounds, all on 3x gut and all but the last on one tackle. The original tackle was chewed to bits by the first pike, who (after a little trouting net had collapsed under him) was landed with all the hooks but one broken. The spare tackle was chewed up by his smaller cousin so effectually that, having no other, I had to go home and be in time for supper, an astonishing mishap, breaking all precedents. Yesterday's bag was lighter but stranger, for it included, besides three trout and a perch, a couple of sizeable eels. The eels, I hasten to explain, were not caught on a spinning minnow, though they might have been, for once in Sussex a big eel grabbed a Holroyd spinner that was searching a pool for pike. The first was caught almost by accident, the second of set purpose to prove that the accident could be repeated.

The river was extremely clear. I was on the wrong side of it, with the sun behind me, because at this point it was impossible to move along the other bank. Consequently I had a clear view of a wide stretch of river bottom. I had fumbled a cast unforgivably and my minnow (not a very fresh one) had sunk to the bottom and caught in a stone. I waded up till I was opposite to it, when, pulling sideways, I was able to release it. Just as it came free I noticed the waving motion of an eel not far from it which, when it had gone, seemed to be looking for it. Presently the eel dropped down-stream and disappeared. I wondered whether the minnow had dropped near him or whether he had scented it from far away. So I dropped the minnow in again and let it rest on the bottom between two stones. Wedging my rod under my arm I pulled out a box of matches to light my pipe, but before I had struck a match, I saw an eel, the first or another, moving in wide zigzags up the river. He moved first to one side, then to the other, in gradually narrowing casts, which brought him between me and the minnow. The moment he was above the minnow, his whole manner changed. The current no longer brought the smell of it to him. At once he dropped below it and again began quartering the ground, like a dog picking up a scent. This time his zigzags were much shorter and he soon found the minnow. He examined it a moment, then seized it between the hooks of the spinning tackle, which, as they were bright, I could see on either side of his jaws. He proceeded to swim away with it, down-stream, when I struck, hooked him and, with little rod bent double, tried to remember what to do with eels. Netting, of course, was out of the question. I slid him ashore, got a foot on him and, before he had time to do damage, beheaded him with a Finnish knife won in a Swedish lottery and never before of any use but obviously intended for the prompt despatch of eels. I put another damaged minnow in again a few yards higher up and the performance was exactly repeated by another eel who, like the first, is at this moment in the frying-pan.

The episode illustrated the more amiable side of the life of the eel, and it was a little unfair that he, who has so many vices, should fall a victim to one of his virtues. Destructive as he is of spawn and fry, he is a notable scavenger. Those eels of yesterday made no attempt, in sunlight, to pursue the shoals of living minnows. But a dead minnow, it was clear, would not have been allowed to pollute the stream for many minutes. At dusk and at night, the eels would no doubt have been busy in a less meritorious manner. A yearling trout would have small chance if even a small eel had once got a grip of it in those disproportionately powerful jaws. I do not suppose that anyone will set out with spinning tackle systematically to fish for eels. But, at the end of a day, when minnows are past their prime, a fisherman with a taste for experiment, will find some interest in watching the eel searching for the bait, some excitement when he has hooked him in preventing him from getting his tail round a snag, and finally will learn that stewed or fried eel is delightful, if he does not know that already. Fished in this way the eel cannot adopt his usual loathsome custom of swallowing the hook. The only real danger is that the angler may rashly lift him in the air when, treating himself as a pro-longation of the line, your eel will tie knots in himself with incredible rapidity, passing the knots up the line as fast as he ties them, and making such a tangle as will put a stop to fishing. Eels call, on capture, for swift action, firmness of character and a Finnish knife.

'The One That Got Away'

The sea-trout rushed across the pool while the reel screeched. At different moments I saw a long greenish flash in the water, a tail, a shoulder. But he never jumped, never came up and splashed. By all the signs I took it that he was well hooked. As for his weight, I could feel it. As for what he was, had I not seen a shoal of the fish in that very pool an hour before when prospecting from among the trees on the high bank? He drove forcibly about the pool, while I settled down to the routine business of tiring him out. Only once he frightened me by getting a rock between us. Then, suddenly, he began to go down-stream. Before I could move on the slippery stones he was below me. I hurried after him, but not fast enough, and presently he was nearing the rapids leading to the next pool, which, from my side of the river can only be reached with great difficulty. I backed ashore and put on all the strain I could in hope of pulling him across into quieter water. This was extremely foolish. Again and again I have tricked a fish into coming up by slackening pressure on him. On this occasion the run down-stream was so sudden that it startled me into folly. And then, the hook pulled out and I had lost him as I deserved. I was too sorry to keep this misadventure to myself when I met my companion. 'How big?' said he. Now I know my rod well and the feel of a fish on it. I had seen enough to know that this fellow was not foul-hooked. Speaking to myself, I put that fish down as from three to four pounds. Until I lost him I had put him at four at least. But so many lies have been told about fish that it has become, in such cases, almost uncomfortable to tell the truth. For my companion, I estimated that departed mort at about a couple of pounds. That would be easier for him to believe. But, even so, I had asked too much and I felt that his condolences were a concession. Driving home, with the bitter knowledge that I had lost a four-pound fish and that even by cutting down his weight by half I had failed to make him altogether credible, I reflected with a good deal of resentment on the reasons that have brought people to describe as 'fishy' any statement in which they do not believe.

For at least 275 years the honesty of fishermen has been something questionable. It should be noted that Izaak Walton, whose book was published in 1653, spoke not of 'anglers *and*' but of 'anglers *or* very honest men'. Walton, of course, would have censured me for saying that I 'lost' a sea-trout which I never had, except pulling mightily at the end of my line. He would also have censured me for describing as approximately two pounds weight a fish, lost or not lost, which I believed to be four. But he would have understood that my dishonesty in diminution was not an original sin but a by-product of a great many other people's dishonesty in exaggeration. For too many years not all but too many fishermen have had 'a multiplying eye'. They have lied in words. They have lied in gesture. I think of that apparently involuntary, horizontal and centrifugal motion of the hands that inspired Mr Punch's picture of a scarecrow addressed by an angler returning from a club dinner with the words, 'My d . . . d . . . dear fellow, I d . . . d . . . don't believe you!' We none of us do, and disbelief of what is implied by that gesture has become so general that even the most honest fishermen are unpleasantly conscious of it. Even for them that natural and beautiful gesture has been spoilt. Nowadays, if you closely observe a man who by that motion of his hands is explaining to another the size of a fish, you will see that his hands have a nervous tendency to close again, especially if the other man looks steadily upon them. The fish would seem to be elastic and, having stretched, to discover, suddenly, a willingness to shrink.

I think that men tell lies about fish not so much from boast-

114

fulness, as is generally supposed, as from stiffness of mind. For there is no denying that the actual business of fishing is one of deception. When you offer a trout a bundle of silk and feathers you tell him, as well as your skill allows you, that it is a pleasantly edible fly. You hope that he will not find out that you are lying until it is too late. When you offer a roach a maggot you hide from him as far as you can your intention to pull him from the water by means of it. Your ground-bait, the half-dozen hookless maggots flung in from time to time, are so many false asseverations that the maggot on your hook is equally harmless. Now it is not your naturally deceitful but your stiff-minded man who cannot keep his falsehood in the proper place, who cannot without extraordinary effort tell lies to fish, but truth to men. It is stiff-mindedness, not wickedness, for there is nothing to be gained by it. You will find that the more noted liars among your fishing acquaintance are men with a marked lack of nimbleness of mind, no splitters of hairs, the sort of men who apply particular names in a general sense, who call, for example, everyone a Bolshevik who does not vote for the Conservative party. They are not romancers but simply dull fellows and probably bad fishermen. They are likely even to lie to themselves in their own fishing diaries. It is these dull fellows, a few of them in every generation, who have brought all talk about fishing to such a lamentable pass.

Good fishermen know that in talking about fishing nothing is interesting except the truth. Of what use is it to us to hear that B. lost a five-pounder in a certain pool when we know that five may mean two or one and that pounds in this connection are not registered weights, but vary in the most incalculable manner. It comes simply to this, that B. tells us that he lost a fish and that he puts it at five pounds because he does not expect us to believe him anyway. Neither party gets any satisfaction. Of course it does not matter at all that we should be disbelieved by the main herd of humanity who, not being fishermen, can hardly be said to be more than partially alive.

There is no need to talk to them on matters obviously above their heads. But it is sad that owing to the dull and stiff-minded members of our own high order we cannot talk to each other with confidence that we shall be believed. When a big fish gets away the truth about it lies, if not at the bottom of a well, at the bottom of a pool in the river. There is no getting at it except on rare occasions. To speak of it is to ask a man to believe an unlikely thing on uncorroborated evidence; unlikely because many more small fish are caught than big; uncorroborated, because it is impossible to weigh the fish. Yet there is no point in lying on such a matter. It is no honour to have lost a fish. If we speak of it, it is to seek sympathy, not praise. Yet, thanks to a few liars in every generation, we risk the insult of mere politeness. In general, perhaps, it would be better to say nothing about lost fish. But, when you are still smarting with the loss, still in the mood of Lucifer first dumped in Hell (for there are few more violent shocks than that with which a man playing a good fish finds that he is playing nothing at all), it is almost impossible to keep quiet about it.

A Day of Small Things

Those know little of the pleasure of angling who imagine that it is measurable in terms of fish, whether in the water or out of it, or that its degrees correspond to different kinds of fish. A day's salmon fishing is not intrinsically better than a day after trout; a day after trout is not necessarily better than a day after grayling and, in pleasure alone, a day after very small things may far surpass the day on which you caught your biggest fish, or made your proudest basket.

Yesterday there was hardly any water in the upper reaches of the little river which I mostly fish. It is a rocky, tumbling little river, but a few miles lower-down flows sedately through the sandflats to join the estuary. Below the point at which it puts off childish things, stops babbling and begins to resemble a rather tortuous canal there are pike, and these pike, we have come to think, take toll of the up and down traffic of fish better than themselves. Another river, free from pike and only a mile or so away, has a respectable run of sea-trout, whereas we have very few and for some time now, trout-fishers have been making it a point of honour now and then to go down-stream to the still waters where the pike lie and to take a few out by spinning for them. Their places, however, seem to be filled by others as soon as they are empty, and though no one has caught a big pike there, no one has hitherto failed to bring away a number of little ones. In that part of the stream there are hardly any trout. There are said to be roach, but I have not seen any. The run of trout up and down the river has its times and seasons, and since the pike are always there, they must feed on something else. It has been suggested that they live on each other, but there are too many of them for that. So, yesterday being a day that promised nothing in the way of trout-fishing, I went, for the first time, far down the little river, to do my duty in removing small pike and, if possible, to find out what they lived on. I took with me a short spinning rod, a Malloch, a roach rod, a quill float, a couple of fine casts, a couple of spinners, a spinning cast, some No. 16 barbless hooks, a tin of maggots from Manchester and a box of worms from a heap of damp sacking placed to attract them in a shady corner of the garden. This, by the way, is the best and cleanest of all methods of keeping up a summer supply of worms. The worms come up into the sacking and make themselves at home there and, when you need them, you fold it back and pick those you think the likeliest.

I came to the river sunk, like a deep ditch, in the flat sandy pastures above the estuary. The water was brown and smooth and silent. Here and there it was fringed by rank weed but, at first, I could see no sign of fish life of any kind. I thought that perhaps I had come below the limits of the pike country, the upper boundary of which is clearly marked and known to all who fish the river. Perhaps I had reached the tidal water. But, just as I was turning to go further up, I thought I saw a V-shaped wave shoot out from the bank, pass up-stream and into the bank again. If that was a pike, he must be living on something. So I chose the deepest hole I could find (not more than four feet at its deepest), put three Manchester maggots on a hook and, for a few minutes, fished carefully. Nothing happened. I wondered if the gentle, fitful up-stream wind had not tricked me into seeing that wave. So I balanced the roach rod on my basket, put up the spinning rod, with an old india-rubber wagtail, blue, silver and red, touched up with green where the paint had worn away, and, casting up-stream (for there was not room to cast across), went slowly along the bank. At the third cast, just where the wave had gone into the bank, there was a jerk at the rod-top, a pale flash in the brown water and presently a lively little jack was netted out. Before reaching the

top of the field I had missed one, seen another follow my wagtail to the bank and lie there looking up at me malignantly, as
only pike can look, and caught a fellow to the first. The water
had shallowed to six inches and there was a muddy dyke by the
hedge, so I turned and went back to my roach rod. The float
had gone. I pulled and found I was fast in the bottom. The
wagtail on the stout pike line served as a grapnel and brought
up the branch of a tree, intricately enlaced. Ten minutes' hard
work disentangled it. I baited and threw out again, went down-
stream about the same distance and got two more small jack.
By the time I got back, the float was gone again and the line
twisted in and out of an underwater weed in a way that almost
showed me the eel, going tail first, round and round and in and
out until he could free himself. Having done my duty by the
river in removing four jack and being extremely hot, I settled
down, put on a purple headed worm and determined to see
that eel if I had to wait till dark. I had not to wait so long. The
float dipped a quarter of an inch, dipped again, went just under
water and jigged there. I struck, and there was my eel, pulling,
as eels do, like fish four times their size. He was given Chinese
execution in the usual way and, easily removing the barbless
hook, I put a rather larger worm on it. The float stood motionless for some ten minutes, then dipped violently and went
down and away. This time, instead of the steady *andante* of the
eel's pull, there was a sharp *staccato*. Long before I saw its
scarlet fins and olive bars I knew it for what it was and landed
a jolly alderman of a perch of 10 oz. astonishing from this ditch
where I had not known they existed, and good for anywhere in
the district. Just then two rabbits came from their burrows in
the sandy opposite bank, and sat motionless for half an hour,
watching me. At the end of that time one of them scratched his
neck with his hind-leg. That showed a profound increase in
confidence and thereafter, until I got up to pack my things and
go, the rabbits fed, pausing only when I lifted my rod to cast
or to bring a fish to bank. A huge flock of rooks passed over.

Peewits called. Hidden in the deep bank of the river I was below the level of the fields, isolated from the world except for the two rabbits, the opposite bank, twenty yards of brown stream and the blue sky overhead. There was none of the lively, changing scenery of trout-fishing. Nor did I catch much. Another half-pound perch, a little one put back, and three more eels at decent intervals punctuated the afternoon. Four little jack, four small eels and a brace of perch, and yet what with the rabbits, the absolute stillness, the surprise of finding my little trout stream giving this kind of fishing, one of the most delightful days of this or any year.

Fast and Loose Fish

The laws of whaling, said Herman Melville, 'might be engraven on a Queen Anne's farthing or the barb of a harpoon and worn round the neck, so small are they: — I, A Fast-Fish belongs to the party fast to it. II, A Loose-Fish is fair game for anybody who can soonest catch it. But what plays the mischief with this masterly code is the admirable brevity of it, which necessitates a vast volume of commentaries to expound it.'

The grave difficulty in the application of this code lies in the infinite variety of states in which a fish may be, between the definitely fast and the indisputably loose. And this same difficulty, the cause of many quarrels between whalers on the high seas, exists for less adventurous fishermen who with rod and line pursue a similar but more delicate craft in less tremendous scenes. Scarce a book has been written on fishing without its contribution to these commentaries, its example or precedent to be brought forward, like an old law case, to settle riverside argument. The best known, the most often quoted, is that in the *Compleat Angler*. 'Oh, me!' exclaims Piscator, 'he has broke all: there's half a line and a good hook lost.' Venator: 'Ay, and a good trout too.' Piscator: 'Nay, the trout is not lost, for pray take notice, no man can lose what he never had.' If a man lose a hook and a cast in a fish and another man capture that fish he will not surrender it, but may take occasion to return, in public, his hook and line to the less fortunate angler. So the other day, after I had explained that I had lost a hook to green gut in a large perch, did my companion, an hour later, hand me a very small perch with my hook and gut plainly to be recognized in its mouth, with the suggestion that I might get them out and use them again. The hook and the humiliation were to be mine, but there was no question as to who should count the little perch into his catch. Then there are many cases of fish departing with one angler's tackle and being brought to bank by another who had been skilful enough to hook the trailing line. All these cases are simple enough. There are others, far more subtle, in which equity would seem (though only seem) to deny the validity both of Melville's whaling code and of Walton's philosophical statement.

Once upon a time I was fishing down a salmon pool, spinning a small shrimp. I had nearly reached the tail of the pool when I saw a salmon swirl under my shrimp, roll over, and disappear without touching it. 'Aha, my lad,' said I, 'you and I are going to know each other better.' I made another cast, and then, marking the ground with my heel, prepared to go back ten or twenty yards and to spin over that ground carefully again, with some confidence that the interest of that salmon had been stirred and that in one of the next few casts the shrimp would be grabbed by him as it swung round. I looked round to see standing close by me a large, benevolent, happy clergyman, who had evidently been watching my proceedings. 'This looks a good pool,' said he; 'I think I will fish it.' He had in his hand a salmon rod and from the end of his cast dangled a fine red prawn. Now, was I to claim the right to fish once more over the salmon I had interested or was I, having fished down once, to surrender the pool to him? I hesitated for a moment, and then sat down to watch. He threw out his prawn creditably enough, and presently approached the mark I had made in the ground. Just as he reached it, he flung up his rod with tremendous violence. A salmon – my salmon – had neatly removed the prawn from between the hooks. The happiness and excitement of the clergyman were like limelight about his portly person. But, he explained, that was his only prawn. What could I do but open my glycerine bottle and give him one of mine? He went down the pool again and yet again,

but my salmon would have no more of him, and at last, tiring
of the splash of what was now his prawn in what had been my
place, I moved away, thinking of the law of Fast-Fish and
Loose-Fish and wondering into which category should properly
be set a salmon which a man has evidently roused from apathy.
A Fast-Fish he is not. But is it fair to consider him wholly
Loose?

On the whole, looking at the matter in cool blood, I think
that the clergyman was within his rights; that, as he arrived at
the pool when I was nearing the bottom of it after fishing it
down, he could properly assume that I should leave it to him
to do the same. After he had fished it, I have no doubt, he
would have given it up if I had wished it. Further, if he had
caught my salmon, I should have had no cause for complaint
whatever. I had had a chance of catching it and had not caught
it. I think that we both behaved quite well, but that, in those
particular circumstances, it was more difficult for me to be
virtuous than for him. And, after all, difficult virtue is something of a pleasure in itself. If I had insisted on fishing over
that salmon again and had caught it, I should have felt rather
a pig. It would have weighed on my conscience as well as on
my shoulder-strap. I was decidedly better without it. For there
is a law of fair angling which does not come into Melville's
whaling code and that is that where the possibility of turning
Loose-Fish into Fast-Fish is shared it should be shared as
evenly as possible. The worst of fishing crimes is to diminish
another fisherman's chances, except, of course, by catching
the biggest fish in the river. There was once a fly-fisher who,
after fishing a favourite pool, used to stone it. I have read of
men in a roach-fishing competition who used their ground-bait
in such a way that, though it might not bring fish to themselves, it prevented them from coming into the swims of their
neighbours. But these be monsters, not men. I am happy to
say I have never met such mean-spirited creatures. When
fishermen sin in this way they sin from thoughtlessness, like

the man I saw but yetserday who marched, with a huge rod
perpendicular over his head, close to the edge of the water
down a pool up which I was slowly working after trout. There
are always fish along that bank, and by keeping well out of
sight below them it is sometimes possible to take them. I had,
in fact, taken two before I was petrified by the sight of this
marching figure. I protested mildly, when he calmly said that
the fish were accustomed to it. If so, they are accustomed to
the sight of bad fishermen. He then added insult to injury by
waiting to watch me fish fruitlessly up the length that he had
spoiled. Not until I reached the point from which he had
started his parade did I begin to catch fish again. Either he was
an habitual worm-fisher by muddy waters or it simply had not
occurred to him that, whether you are fishing or not, you are
sinning against unwritten law when you warn the Loose Fish
in the river that there are those about who seek to make them
Fast.

Carp

August and September are the best in the year for carp-fishing, and it is pleasant to turn to the carp from such fish as trout and salmon which put a less insistent strain upon the nerves. But not too often. A man who fishes habitually for carp has a strange look in his eyes. I have known several and have even shaken hands respectfully with the man who caught the biggest carp ever landed in England. He looked as if he had been in heaven and in hell and had nothing more to hope from life, though he survived, and after six years caught an eighteen-pounder to set beside the first. Carp-fishing combines enforced placidity with extreme excitement. You may, day after day, for weeks watch your rod fishing on your behalf (for you do not hold it in your hand), and then, at last, you see your float rise and move off and, striking with proper delay, are suddenly connected to the fastest fish that swims. A salmon keeps it up longer, but I doubt if even he has the carp's appalling pace. Trout are slow, dogged creatures in comparison. Further, carp are immensely strong. To hold them safely you need stout gut, but to use stout gut is to throw away most chances of having a carp to hold. There is something terrifying about these fish. To hook a big one is like being jerked out of bed by a grapnel from an aeroplane. Their speed, size and momentum are enhanced, in their effect upon the mind, by the smallness and stillness of the ponds in which they are to be found. The pleasantest such place I know is the lake in front of a tower that Cromwell burnt, a placid pool where frogs spawn in Spring, with ancient trees on the still more ancient dam that holds it up. These trees have, during the storms of several centuries, dropped branch after branch into the lake and the bottom there is rich with decaying leaves and fortresses for fish. You cast out and pray (1) that you may not hook an oak bough, and (2) that if you hook a carp he may neglect the snags on either side of him and give you just a slightly better chance of catching him by burying himself in the water-lilies in the middle of the lake. You cast out, I say. Alas, there is no longer anything to cast for. The lake was drained for its fish during the war, and the men who took them took even finger-lings and left nothing alive that they could see. The carp in that lake, however, did not run very large. There were a few big ones killed when it was drained, but nothing of the size I saw at the week-end in a duck-pond that could scarcely have covered two acres. This pond was square and used for washing sheep. There was a little wooded island in it and a sunken willow tree. Its banks were almost without bushes. It was simply a shallow bath-tub of a pond. It had not even water-lilies. It looked as if it had no fish. When I came to the pond side, I believed I had been misled and was consoled by watching a flock of wild Canada Geese resting beside it. For some minutes they took no notice of me; then, all together, twelve or thirteen of them, they raised their long black necks and, a moment later, rose into the air, cleared the hedge and, lifting slowly, flew away. I was still watching them when I heard something like a cart-wheel fall into the pond. Huge rings showed, even on the wind-swept surface. I watched for a particularly clumsy diving bird to come up again. None came, but, just as a gleam of sunshine opened the racing clouds, there was another vast splash and a huge, pale gold fish rose into the air, shook himself in a cloud of spray, gilded by the sunshine and his own colour in the midst of it, and fell heavily back into the water.

In a few minutes after that the rods were up and the baits cast out (with the helping wind it was easy to get them well out towards the middle of the lake). The floats were adjusted so as to lie on the surface, held by the resting shot, while the bait with a couple of feet of fine gut lay on the bottom. The placidity of floats so adjusted is like that of anchored ships. Life has left them. They lie, dead, on the top of the water. They do not drift. There is no feeling that they may be approaching a fish. All that can be hoped is that down below, on the mud, a fish is approaching them. The fisherman can do no more. A yard or two of line lies on the ground beside his reel. Until that line is drawn out he must do nothing. He is immobilized, while tremendous events impend. Chained hand and foot, he waits on destiny. And destiny, rumbling here and there with terrific splashes of golden leviathans, makes havoc of his nerves. He cannot, like the trout fisher, find expression and relief in lengthening his line and casting over a rise. He must steel himself to leave his rod alone and this enforced inaction in the exciting presence of huge fish, visibly splashing, produces a sort of drugged madness in the fisherman. I could not keep my hands still, nor could I reply sanely to questions. A true record of the life of an habitual carp-fisher would be a book to set beside De Quincey's *Confessions of an English Opium-Eater*, a book of taut nerves, of hallucinations, of a hypnotic state (it is possible to stare a float into invisibility) of visions, Japanese in character, of great blunt-headed, golden fish, in golden spray, curving in the air under sprays of weeping willow, and then rare moments when this long-drawn-out tautness of expectation is resolved into a frenzy of action. When, at last, I hooked one of these fish, I could not keep in touch with him, though I was using an American multiplying reel with which, on a trout rod, I have kept easily in touch with a salmon. Again and again, he won yards of slack and yet, when he was landed, he was no glass-case fish, but quite an ordinary carp, which, at the end of the day I put back into the pond. For carp-fishing, it was a lucky day. Four times the baits were taken by eels, landed amid anathemas, tempered by the thought of next day's breakfast. Four times they were taken by carp. One fish was landed. Twice the carp shot off with such speed that the reel over-ran, checked and gave him warning. On the fourth occasion one of the monsters made a direct run of thirty yards and then broke me, the fine gut cast parting above the float. There then occurred an incident that illustrates the uncanny nature of these fish. My float, lying out in the middle of the pond, turned and sailed slowly in again to my very feet, towed by the monster who then in some manner freed himself, thus returning me my tackle with a sardonic invitation to try again. No other fish is capable of putting so fine a point on irony.

The Salmon-fishers

At night the salmon-fishers were talking with great hope of the morrow.

Breakfasts were a little furtive. The genial, collective hopefulness of the night had narrowed into partitions. Each man nursed his private optimism over his coffee and bacon and eggs in the big dining-room of the inn. The servants of that inn have great experience. They never ask what sport a man has had when he returns from the river, but, in the morning, as they take orders for sandwiches, they contrive to make the fisherman feel that they believe his unexpressed optimism is perfectly justified. No word is said, but the brisk handling out of a neat parcel of sandwiches may be itself eloquent. Each man goes off to the river enveloped in confidence. The cars that carry them seem as eager as spaniels on the morning of a shoot. Engines are never cold and reluctant, as they so often are when they have to take a man to his business. No time is wasted and by half-past nine the whole flock of little cars and big cars outside the inn has vanished like the morning dew.

It is a river of good sportsmanship. There is no balloting for beats, but somehow everyone has morning or afternoon in his favourite pool. There are pools and to spare and in the whole club there is but one man who is greedy, tries to fish more than his share, hurries from pool to pool, and is suspected of worse things. He is tolerated and perhaps useful. His horrible example sets by contrast an even higher standard for his fellow-members. The humane arrangement of the fishing means that at luncheon, in the middle of the day, there is much meeting between fishermen leaving one beat and going to another. Few luncheons are eaten in solitude and hopes that have waned during the morning are rekindled. 'Did you touch anything?' 'Rose one by the willow.' 'He's mine this afternoon.' 'Good luck to you. Did you see much?' 'There were half a dozen showing in the Stakes, but it's a plaguey bit of casting to reach them.' The fish are there, right enough. The water is a good height. The man who has not fished a pool thinks that perhaps his casting may just do the trick for him, or he will ask what flies the other fished. 'What flies? Half a dozen. Thunder and Lightning was what I had on first. I changed to a Jock when the sun came out and then to a smaller Jock, and then a Bull-Dog and after that a Silver Doctor.' 'You didn't try a Butcher?' 'I hadn't one with me.' The fisherman who is going to that pool in the afternoon looks at the Butchers in his box, discusses the question of size and is already convinced that the Butcher, his Butcher, is the fly for which the fish are waiting.

We separate and go off in couples to our afternoon pools. The fish are showing. A huge fellow, dull silver with a bloom over him, leaps clear of the water. Another turns over, showing flank and mighty tail. A little one, eight or ten pounds, comes up and goes under again, not quite clearing the water but forging through its surface for a moment. Steadily we work down the pool. That cast, the lift, the use of the water's pull to give a catapult release for the backward throw, the straightening of the line up the river, the half-turn over of the rod and the outward flick – all these things combined in clockwork motion are easier than they were last year and much easier than they were this morning. But still the salmon show immediately above the water we are fishing and immediately below. Up they come to look the fisher in the face. But they leave his flies alone and the fisher is already busy on a new alchemy. He had persuaded himself that afternoon is better than morning. He is now persuading himself that, after all, the catching of a salmon is the least part of fishing. The open air is a delight and so is the feeling that he can get so much more than usual of it into his lungs as his chest swells and his shoulders widen with even a day's casting. Each successful cast is in itself an end achieved. The salmon-fisher is casting to satisfy himself, not the fish. He is in the position of the artist who must be his own critic. The salmon is the reader or listener who may or may not overhear him and after all applauds, when he does applaud, not a fine piece of casting, but the inessential fly. Such are the dialectics whereby, as the afternoon draws on, the fisher fortifies himself against a blank day.

By the end of September, days are drawing in fast and there is already no temptation to be late for dinner. The sun sinks behind the clouds over the hills. Once more we go carefully down the pool. Then one last cast at 'the taking place' and we reel up, wade ashore for the last time, take off the last fly of the many we have wet this day, take down the rod for easy carrying and walk together down the river to the fishing hut, talking lightly of otter and heron and the beauty of the evening sky, of everything but salmon. In the pool above the hut a man is casting busily, with a landing net on his shoulder, trying for sea-trout. 'Why do you go for rabbits when there are lions about?' says my companion rashly. 'How many lions have you caught?' comes the reply, and we do not dare to ask him for his tale of rabbits.

At the inn they are comforting each other with reports of woe. 'At least,' says my companion, 'if we haven't got any, no one else has, and I don't believe there was a salmon to be caught today.' That is the key-note of dinner, which is a far humaner and more genial meal than breakfast. We soothe our self-respect with the knowledge of general failure. You would think that our view was the salmon's, exulting that none of his kind has fallen to the wiles of man. And then somebody notices that not all of us are here. The two — the brothers, have not been at dinner. 'One of them,' says somebody, 'is into a fish, and the other is lighting a fire on the bank to land him by.' 'Not a bit of it,' says somebody else. 'They're still having last casts.' We go out into the dark street. A car is at the door and from it one of the brothers is unpacking rods and waders. The other is invisible. 'Yes,' says the visible brother, glowing under the lamp in the porch, 'he hooked one just as we going to come away, and it played pretty hard and took him down a couple of hundred yards.' 'Did he get it?' 'Yes. A twenty-pounder and a bit over.' And with that there is a revolution in everybody's feelings. Our dialectics are swept off like cobwebs. There is great joy for the lucky fisherman, whom everybody likes, and we need no more philosophy. Man holds his own again. The fish are there and the fish are to be caught. This night, like last, the salmon fishers are talking with great hope of the morrow.

Seeing or Believing?

This year, the Lune seems likely to miss the crowning glory of its autumn colouring. The sharp night frosts have already brought many of the leaves from the trees before they have wholly lost the green of summer and before they have caught the golds and reds and oranges with which, as a rule, they flare up before being quenched for the winter. Today the water was low and so clear that it was possible in all but the fastest streams to watch the leaves rolling along the bottom, or drifting in mid-water. To these conditions I owe an experience that I am not likely to repeat. On account of the low bright water I was spinning with the lightest possible tackle, what is known as a 2x line and a very light 8-foot 6-inch trout rod. My minnow was not heavily weighted, and I could watch it the whole time it was spinning and, almost always, help it to dodge the leaves.

Below the foot bridge is a rocky gorge with several deep holes and strong current. Below these again is a true pool, with a narrow, fastish entrance, a steady slightly curling stream down the middle which affects all the water except a strip of slack at either side. From the rocks at the neck, I thought I saw something move among the stones on the bottom near the middle of the pool. I threw my minnow into the slack water on the far side, spun it into the edge of the stream and then let it swing, spinning slowly, over the place where I thought I had seen a fish. As it came towards my side of the pool a big fish rose from under it and swung with it, a foot below it, but did not take. With that a miracle seemed to have been worked upon the pool. The passage of the minnow at that place seemed in some way to have excited more fish than the one that followed it. Two others appeared as if from nowhere and, I think, a fourth. One after another they did a corkscrew curl deep in the pool. Head up-stream and tail down, they twirled over sideways. They moved continually in a space of not more than a few yards. I put the minnow over them again and it was as if they had been dancing a slow quadrille and the music had suddenly quickened. The minnow came into the still water and I brought it up fast and threw it out again, putting the rod well out to keep the minnow hanging as long as possible over this ball-room of blue and green crystal. There was a frenzy under water, great shapes moving round, getting out of each other's way, but still not taking. The river watcher told me in the evening that he had seen a similar mad dance when fishing with a prawn in a clear deep pool at his feet. The swirl of a moving fish broke the surface. For a moment I could not see fish or minnow and in that moment I saw my line describe a half-circle outwards at the point where it entered the water. I lifted the little rod. For a few seconds I felt a steady strain. Then the reel buzzed like a wasp in a spider's web and I was scrambling over the rocks, making the best going I could in waders and brogues, to get below my fish. When I had got below him he was away on the other side of the pool. I could see him and he seemed a very little one. For one moment I thought he was a sea-trout foul-hooked, so much less did he seem than the partners of the strange dance I had observed. He came up and broke water, as if to restore my respect for him. He was a good salmon, not a big one, but well over ten pounds. He went fast up the middle of the stream. I thanked him for that, but too soon. Down he came again and as he passed through some bright smooth water I thought I saw another fish with him. But he gave me no time to make sure, coming down on the far side of one of those long sharp edged rocks that rise from the bed of the river. That had to be stopped and for a moment it seemed too late to stop it. Giving him very little strain, just keeping taut and no more so as not to help him

134

to cut the line, I got above him, cleared the line and getting below him again tricked him into moving and with a side strain got his head athwart the stream. He was already near the tail of the pool. Obviously he would have to go down to the pool below. I struggled down ahead of him just in time to save the line as he slipped through the rapids into a deep narrow pool like those immediately below the bridge. I could not hold him here either and we shot another cataract together. Again I had had an impression that he was not alone. Now, in a piece of glass clear water I could see that he was not. With him was a much larger salmon. My salmon got his nose down against a rock, and while he was trying to free himself there and I was trying to get him moving, this other larger salmon stood by. My salmon found the side strain too much for him and slipped down a few yards. The other salmon came with him. Then occurred the incident on account of which I am writing this paper. My salmon was holding his own against the current, low in the water. The other salmon was circling round the line (I describe what I thought I saw at the time) and, after doing this several times, suddenly let himself be swept broadside on against the cats immediately above my salmon's head. My distance from the two fish would be about five yards. I felt suddenly a new weight on my rod and could see the cast strained round the larger salmon at a point some foot and a half above the minnow which I could see equally plainly hanging at my salmon's mouth. The whole incident lasted only a moment. Both fish swept down. The big fish rolled off my line and the story ended with my salmon letting me gaff him and lift him out. But though he was a nice fish, weighing close on fifteen pounds when he was weighed later in the day, my interest was already not in him but in his big companion. Did the big fish consciously try, in that most practical manner, to help his fellow to escape. Did I have the extraordinary good fortune to witness that? Or did he, out of curiosity alone, follow him down two pools and, while looking at him, suddenly feel the touch of the line and so be moved to that sudden gesture that looked exactly as if he had, on purpose, flung the whole weight of himself against the line? Was it seeing or believing? At the time, as I sat sweating on the bank beside my salmon, I had no doubts at all. It was only afterwards that I began to look for other explanation than purpose in the fish. I realize now that if my best friend had told me that tale I should have looked him very squarely in the eyes. Dozens of times, of course, fishermen have seen their fish accompanied almost to landing net or gaff. But I know of no other instance of anything that could seem, as this most certainly did seem, to be an attempt at rescue. And I am sure that I may fish for the rest of my life in water as low and clear as was the Lune today without seeing anything like this again.

Coarse-fishing Country

There are coarse fish everywhere, except in those places where
men have been allowed to save their private pockets by
poisoning the public water. But there are some counties in
which, when men speak of fishing, coarse fishing is meant,
counties in which roach and bream, carp and tench, perch and
pike are not the tolerated second cousins, the poor relations of
the trout and salmon, but have things all their own way and
yield precedence to none. We have pike and perch in plenty
in the Lake Country, but few fish for them who can fish for
trout. There is magnificent coarse fishing in Shropshire, but
trout are there also. Neither Shropshire nor the Lake Country,
nor any of the land that lies between them, can be considered
the exclusive domain of those fish which, having no adipose
fins, submit, disdainfully, to being called 'coarse', even by
those who prize them at their proper worth. That exclusive
realm of theirs is the country south of the Humber and east of
the last hills.

They flourish in sluggish waters and do not love the stony-
bottomed rivers which hurry down the steep valleys where the
rocks are near the surface of the soil. The trout and salmon
fisher thinks of Scotland and the north as his own country. The
coarse fisher thinks of a land so unlike this that it is difficult to
believe that they can both be parts of the same island. I came
to that country by way of Leeds, leaving the great trout rivers,
Lune, Ribble, and Wharfe, in flood and working eastwards to
the valley of the Trent. The Trent is not what it used to be,
though, if the polluters will give it a chance, it may again become what it was in the days when J. W. Martin wrote his
delightful books about its barbel, chub, and pike. After crossing

the Trent it was almost as if I had crossed the North Sea.
There were the square sails of barges moving before the wind
among the rain-soaked crops. Here and there were windmills.
The road ran along the top of a dyke above a canal where the
ripples of fish turning on the surface continually invited me to
stop. And so to Brigg and the Ancholme, where the Sheffield
men ply the little light rods, the 'toothpick' floats, and the
lightly shotted casts that are so strange a contrast to the heavy
shotting and the long cork-covered floats of the men of
Nottingham, a contrast strange only to those who have not
compared the waters where these styles developed. Who that
has read it can forget old Martin's description of the great
float that was made for him, to carry a dozen shot and two big
pike leads? But that float was for the fishing of a swim twenty-
five and thirty feet deep in water where less lead would have
failed to keep the bait to the bottom. Here in the Ancholme a
single shot is enough, and that is carried near the float, so that
the bait, instead of being forced downwards, sinks slowly at its
own speed, the only solid mouthful in a cloud of rapidly
evanescent ground bait. The Ancholme was in flood, and,
though it was possible to take fish in it in the Trent style, I saw
some Sheffield men turn from it in dudgeon, to ply their
special craft in some ponds nearby.

From the Ancholme, where, just before the flood, a local
angler landed a golden tench of 4 lb. 10 oz., I turned south to
the Witham and the Welland, through a country absolutely
flat, where the highest mountains are the dykes, where the sky
is as wide and the horizon as level as on the plains of Russia. In
this country, except in the towns, are no large houses. The
cowsheds are the biggest buildings. Travelling hither and
thither about it, from one famous drain or river to another, I
saw in many days outside the towns no single building that
would be described by an auctioneer as a 'gentleman's resi-
dence'. The houses are small, as if those who built them feared
that they might drop through into the mud if they were a

brick or two too heavy. They are small boxes built of brick, often with a weather-proof coating of black tar. They are in keeping with the tradition of the country, the descendants of the huts of the fenmen, hidden here and there with their eel traps among the reeds of the swamps. The swamps have been drained, dykes built, and the fenmen live now on the edges of the drains, no longer in impregnable fastnesses of swamp and water. But this was never a country where it was worth while to own much land. A man wanted room for a hut, a landing-place for his boat, and the whole wilderness of reeds and waters was as much his an anybody else's. The great drains cutting the map in a series of parallel straight lines, the neat roads following the drains for miles along the tops of the imprisoned dykes, give the country now an orderliness that makes it easy to forget how long it survived in wildness parts of England that we still think not wholly tamed. Here are no rivers with babbling shallow, narrow gorge, deep pool, and restful eddy, but streams between banks almost as regular as those of the drains, and with scarcely more motion in them, hundreds of miles of still water, and in it the finest coarse fishing in England. There is no strong water except at flood-time, and very little deep. Wind, not current, dictates the shotting of the cast. Except in a very few places you fish always with mile upon mile of water stretching on either side of you, in appearance exactly like the water before you, between banks exactly like the bank on which you sit. Here is nothing to distract the mind. Here, indeed, is the rigour of the game. Canal fishing, if you like, but canal fishing of superlative quality. The Middle Level Drain, near King's Lynn, where I saw those big bream pulled out a week ago, is like a railway cutting filled with water. So is the Forty Foot. So, in miniature, are the North and South Drove, the Counter Drain, the Hob-hole, the Bell Water, and all these other famous places. From all parts of England men come to fish these waters, and those who have come once come year after year. Nor are the fenmen themselves without great pride in their possession. In Boston, in Spalding, in Surfleet men talk with hushed voices of great tench and bream. In Spalding the local anglers not only return all small ones to the waters, but bring their large ones, carefully lapped in wet cloths, to their secretary, who, if they are not to go into glass cases, turns them into a pond in some gardens belonging to the town, where the fishermen can call upon them and, watching them grow to yet greater weights, recall the glory of their capture. Coarse fish, indeed? There is no place in England where the captured trout can look forward to a pension and such honour in his old age.

Failing to Catch Tench

The tench 'is the most part of the year in the mudde. And he styryth moost in June and July: and in other seasons but lytyll. He is an evyll byter. . . .' He certainly is. Dame Juliana Berners, whose *Treatyse of Fysshinge with an Angle* was published in 1496, knew what she was talking about. He is, indeed, hardly to be caught unless by those who are willing to sacrifice some of the best of the trout season in his honour, which, year by year, I resolve but fail to do. Three years ago I was complaining of failure to catch tench. The moment I could get away from the trout I had gone down into Shropshire to a pool where many and large tench had been caught. I had failed to catch any and had excused myself by the belief that the tench had already gone down into the mud for the winter. This excuse was taken from me by an unkind correspondent who wrote to tell me that he, though fishing further north, was still catching admirable tench. I made good resolutions for 1927. In 1927 also it was difficult to leave the trout until September, and the nearest I came to catching tench was to see some bubbles in some muddy water. It was said that these bubbles showed that the tench were moving. I observed the bubbles with respect and fished with renewed hope for seven or eight hours. But, if the tench were moving, they were not feeding. They may have been shrugging their shoulders. I made good resolutions for 1928. I had heard of a pond in Gloucestershire. . . .

In June of this year I heard again of that pond. It was described as a small pond and very weedy. The tench, said Colonel Venables, writing in 1662, 'chuseth the deepest and stillest place,' 'and also green weeds, which he loveth exceedingly.'

Nor was that all. The owner of the pond, who can hardly be
described as a fisherman (his interests are of a different kind)
had actually been catching tench. He had seen them wallowing
on the shallows in May and, not knowing that they were en-
titled to a close season and that this was it, he had fished for
them with careless confidence and 'pulled out' as many as he
wanted. I have long ago come to think with envy of any man
who can fish for tench with confidence. Still, there it was, a
pond, practically unfished, full of green weeds and tench. I
began to think of it, if not with confidence, at least with hope.
But at that time there was no possibility of getting away from
the trout. There were experiments to be tried with flies, and
Gloucester was far away. Once more it was not until September,
when the trout season had ceased to be interesting, that I
looked out the right floats (Mr Sheringham says that red tops
are essential) and travelled some two hundred miles south-
wards into Gloucestershire to catch some of those tench.

The pond was in the grounds of a house at which Cromwell
is reputed to have rested. It was a typical fish-pond of the kind
made by our ancestors before they became obsessed by adipose
fins, and it is probable that when Cromwell rested at the house
he fed on tench newly taken from it in his honour. Half of it
was fairly open, half shaded by trees. There was a little island
in it, reached by a plank bridge. From this island in the early
summer the owner of the pond had fished for tench and 'pulled
them out' on the sort of tackle that a man is likely to use who,
though he owns a tench pond and a trout stream, prefers
banging about with a gun to a more worthy use of his spare
time. I ought to have felt confident that with fine gut, gilt
hooks and a float with a top of the right tint I was going to
catch one huge tench after another. I did not. Something had
happened to that pond between May and September. Gone
were the green weeds 'which he loveth exceedingly.' Gone
indeed was every weed in the pond and the explanation of this
was swimming contentedly about on the brown muddy water.

To the mistaken delight of the owner, the pond had been the scene of a prodigious multiplication of ducks. There would have been plenty of room on the pond for two, four or even half a dozen ducks and in May, I dare say, there had not been many more. But when I came at last to the pond in the autumn forty or fifty ducks were swimming about on it. More quacked and flapped in the bushes and a small flight of them got up and sailed heavily away over the trees. 'Wild ones,' said my host, evidently very pleased. 'It's an odd thing,' he said, a minute or two later, 'but we haven't seen a sign of those tench for some months.'

Still, one does not travel two hundred miles to fish without fishing. The pond was a delightful place, with excellent cover for a fisherman in the long grass on its firm banks. Three of us, carefully, not to disturb shy fish, crawled to our chosen places. We fished for two days and an evening as well as we knew how. Not one single tench was caught, though, if they were there, they were offered the best of Manchester maggots and some very handsome local worms, hanging on the finest of gut beneath the reddest of small red floats. For the first three or four hours each bob of a float woke eager speculation. After that, we knew. Floats bobbed often enough. Sometimes they sank just a little way. Sometimes they went sharply under as if the worm had been taken by a perch. Once or twice they dipped, slanted and slid off sideways. But, no matter what they did, the reason of their doing it was always the same. I have never caught so many eels in my life.

But the question remains, what had become of the tench? The weather was still warm. They had had no excuse for going down into the mud. Moreover, even if a cold night had sent them down, they could not have gone far, for the pond had a hard bottom not thickly covered. They could hardly have been exterminated by the ducks, though Walton, writing of fish-ponds, warned his readers against leaving the spawn of tench or carp 'to the mercy of ducks or vermin.' The wallowing

143

monsters must have been able to defend themselves from or to evade direct attack. Had the ducks by eating all the weed so far reduced the food supply as to make the pond the scene of a hideous struggle for life between the eels and the tench, in which the tench had starved, died and themselves been eaten, or were the tench still there, lying in the mud at the bottom watching not without satisfaction eel after eel take a dangling worm and presently depart with struggles to an unknown world? With tench you never know. They may still be there but the frosts have come and the falling leaves and tench-fishing in Gloucestershire is over till next year. There is nothing left to be done in the matter of tench, but to make good resolutions for 1929. I have heard of a pond in Nottinghamshire. . . .

My Barbel

I have never fished for barbel. Fishing for barbel needs a greater expenditure of worms and faith than I have ever been in a position to afford. You enrich the river with a thousand lob-worms daily for a week to induce the barbel to look at worms favourably. Then you fish for him. His choice of feeding-places is such that you lose great quantities of tackle in the bottom of the river. But you hardly ever catch a barbel, even after this prodigious baiting. It is a sorry business, persisted in because once or twice in a lifetime an angler finds the barbel on the feed and because no man who has ever caught a barbel can refrain from chanting the praises of this pig – this wild boar, rather – of the river. He is the hardest, most obstinate fighter of any of the coarse fish. Martin has sung his glory, but even he found himself 'wondering whether the game was worth the candle, and how many tens of thousands of worms and stones of boiled scratchings had been dribbled down the barbel swims of various rivers' in vain. Bickerdyke, that most instructive optimist, has told us exactly how to fish for him. But nowadays your true barbel fisher who devotes his life to the pursuit of this strange, strong, bearded bottom-feeder is rare. Barbel-fishing, like mathematical philosophy, has disheartened so many by seeming to lead to nowhere.

Consequently when I went to the Thames, taking one thing with another – the high price of worms, the time of year (far too late), and the extreme unlikelihood of catching any – I decided to leave the barbel alone. I knew the fish were there. But, though a recent guide to the Thames fishing had said of this place and of that, 'Barbel are to be had here,' a deeply experienced Thames fisherman had commented, 'The barbel are there, but they are not to be had. The only thing to be "had" is the fisherman.' So I did not fish for barbel.

Yet in the evening of my last day of Thames fishing I caught one and am compelled, like all the other men who have caught barbel, to pay tribute to him. For it is perfectly true that there is no coarse fish to equal him in prolonged pugnacity and power. He deserves all that has been said in praise of him. Mine was but a moderate barbel (6½ pounds), but he gave me a harder fight than any fish I have ever landed of any species whatever, not excluding salmon. Since it is possible that the same conditions may occur again and that other anglers may similarly catch a barbel at the expense of four seedy lobworms instead of seven thousand good ones, I shall set down in detail how it happened.

I had taken down my tackle and was on my way home along the bank of the river, thinking that my Thames fishing was over and that I should have to be content with a total catch of two Thames trout (returned), some pike, some roach, some dace, some perch, some chub, some gudgeons, two minnows, and a bullhead — none, barring one of the trout, of any remarkable size — when I happened to notice a narrow alley of smooth, slow water close under my own bank. It was a very likely looking roach swim, too good not to try for a minute or two. I had been paternostering for perch and had in my bag no Thames float tackle but only a very small grayling float and a light North-country roach-cast carrying a single shot. There were a few worms left in the bag. I found a depth of four or five feet and sent the tail of a lobworm down the swim. It was taken by a 6-oz. dace. I sent down another. It was taken by a half-pound roach. This was encouraging. I found four dead worms and broke up two and threw them in well above the head of the swim. I sent down the tail of a lobworm again. Close under the bank the float jerked hard under. I thought I was in a weed, and pulled lightly in time to feel a heavy tug and to know that I had lost a fish. I threw in the remaining two dead worms. Now all this time I had never thought of barbel, but, without intent, had been doing what, if I had hoped for a barbel, I might well have done on purpose. For the river had risen a little the day before and was coloured, and in these circumstances say the authorities, barbel leave their deep swims and frequent shallower water. (Bickerdyke, p. 80.) The next time the little float sailed down it came to the place where it had gone under before, passed it, and then went under suddenly and sideways. I struck, and a second later was thanking my stars that the line had not caught, as it often had on that windy day, round a handle of the reel. Instead of pulling a roach to the surface I was in battle with something tugging and boring far out and deep down in the middle of the river. I thought it was a pike, and I expected the bitten gut to come back to me at once. Then, as the fish rushed up-stream, I realized that the manner of his play was not that of a pike. There was no corkscrew, undulate feel about it. It was tugging like a perch, but I knew it was too big for any perch. I thought I had at last got hold of a really big chub. But a chub does not fight for very long, and as the battle continued and I found myself running up the river, for I had no great length of line on my reel, I thought with some resentment, that this was a third Thames trout and that, however big he was, I should have to return him to the water. He went on being a trout for the rest of the battle until, after charging suddenly into the bank and weeding himself, he became a trout of most unusual strength. Up to that moment I had put him down in my mind as a trout of five or six pounds. But then, while he was under my feet in the sedges I felt the hook slip. For about half a second I thought I had lost him, and then out he dashed into the river again, apparently double the size and with four times the energy that he had previously had. I could do nothing with him at all except run after him. We went a hundred yards up the river, and then he turned round and set off for London. Trying to keep below and ahead of him to turn him, I stumbled along in the dusk while he swam deep in the river, now and then jerking the rod down by angry tugs. It grew dark, when, after he had turned twice and gone up river and down again, he began to weaken and allowed me at last to see my float. By this time other fishermen had joined me, but not one of them had a bigger net than my own small trout net. 'That's a big pike you have hold of,' said one. 'It's a quarter of a mile to where you were fishing.' 'It's no pike, but a trout,' said I. And then at last he came to the top and turned over, and we saw the barbules hanging from his lips. I got him into the net and lifted it out by the rim, and there was my $6\frac{1}{2}$ pound barbel with the hook right in the middle of his broad side, about three inches behind the gill covers. The hook fell out when I touched it. I think he had been properly hooked, though lightly, in the beginning, that he had first freed and then foul-hooked himself during the tussle under the bank, that this explained the strange redoubling of his strength, and that, all things considered, I was exceedingly lucky to get him. Next year, I am afraid, be the price of worms what it may, I shall fish for barbel in the orthodox manner, and no doubt be myself sufficiently orthodox not to catch any.

On Talking to the Fish

I wonder whether all fishermen, without knowing it, talk to their fish. When with a companion they seem in talking to him to find relief from an excitement that must otherwise come out in monologue. A gillie I know, says that all the men he has carried a gaff for, swear all the time they have a fish on, with the exception of two parsons. One of these grunts and the other 'talks mush in such a way that if you did not know him you would think he was using bad language'. I have heard a small boy adjuring his float to 'Bob, you brute!' and a small girl who did not like taking fish off the hooks, apologizing to a perch for snatching away the bait which he was visibly on the point of taking. Pike, certainly, are seldom caught in silence. The language used to them is not polite. They look for hostility and are met with it. Many an angler more than half believes that he has heard them answer back. When a pike comes up out of the water, opens his great white mouth and shakes his head, it is hard to believe that he does not actually bark.

A month of two ago I was fortunate in overhearing nearly the whole of the catching of a salmon. I was eating my sandwiches behind a rock when a salmon fisher who did not know I was there came to the head of the pool. There was no one else in sight, and I was startled by hearing him say, not at all below his breath, 'Just by the rock's the place'. He began casting at once and at the second or third cast I heard 'Ha! Looked at it did you? Wondered what museum I'd stolen it from and why I wanted to show it to you? Well, take another look at it. It'll be coming to you in a moment. Now where are you? Hurry up or the gates'll be closed. Last chance of seeing

149

the celebrated Johannes Scotus. ... There you are. ... But why not take the beastly thing? Not good enough for you? Rubbish. Now all the wise men say that I ought to offer you a smaller one of the same. But you and I know better. You want to see this one again. And you shall. Now then. Out of the smooth and into the stream. Are you waiting for it or have you gone off to lament your lack of appetite. Ha. ... One to be ready. Two to be steady. Three to decide that even if he takes it striking is a mug's game and four to ... tighten ... ra ... ther ... FIRMLY.'

At this point the fisherman came down through the shallows at the head of the pool with his rod point well up, his reel screaming and his line taut to something moving rapidly far down the pool. The fisherman hurried over the boulders. 'Would you? Would you?' I heard him ejaculate defiantly, evidently attributing to the fish responsibility for an awkward stumble. He got below his fish and I could see from his lips that he was talking continuously, though I could hear nothing but the stream. I picked up my gaff and, keeping well away from the river went down and took up a position not far from the fisherman, but well out of his way so that I could act as gillie for him if he wanted one. I suppose he must have heard the noise of my arrival, for he looked for half a second in my direction, but he was far too much engrossed in his contest with the fish not to forget my presence almost instantly. He and the fish were alone together. There was no one else in their world.

'Yes, my dear,' I heard him say, 'you are perfectly right. That big stone is the place to make for. Get the line round that and we part company. But I lost a relation of yours round that stone and just for that very reason ... steady now ... I am not going to lose you. No, no, my lad. You're on the wrong side. You should have gone on the other side and got the gut on the sharp edge. What? You think you'll settle down there, do you? Tire me out, eh? We'll see about that. ... Now then. This

150

way with your head, my friend. Just feel the current on your cheek. So. Out you come. Up-stream? De . . . lighted. As far as you want to go. Nothing keeping you. There's sixty yards of backing on this reel. Oh. So you don't want to go any further after all. Well, my dear, you'll have to work hard to keep where you are. There's good strong water coming down there. What? dropping already. You might have had the decency to drop this side of the stream. You can't think that I'm going to lug you across. Now this little backwater here would be just the place to land you. If you won't see it, I can't make you. But . . . look here, if you go much further, you'll have to take a nasty toss into the pool below and I shall have to get down before you. Disobliging brute. Another two yards and there'll be no stopping yourself. Now then, easy, easy. . . .'

The fisherman slid down over the rocks just in time to keep the line clear as the fish rolled through the fall into the low pool. Few things are more astonishing than the gymnastics of which even an elderly man finds himself capable when he has a good fish at the end of his line. The fisherman went down over those rocks like a boy and, with the fish still on, was moving steadily down the low pool before I had had time to make up my mind to follow him. I had no fish to give wings to my feet and took a minute or two to climb down.

I found the conversation still proceeding, though its tone was much less friendly. 'Tired are you, now? No more tricks of that kind. You've spoilt two pools for me. Couldn't you stick to the ring and fight it out handsomely in one. Turning the best pool of the river into a circus. It'll be a couple of hours before it is worth fishing. No, enough of that. You wouldn't come into that backwater. Try this one. So. Another yard. Another foot. What? Not tired yet? Saw the gaff, did you? Didn't like the look of my face. I shouldn't have thought you had that much run left in you. Coming down again now. Turning over. Keep your head up-stream. Round again. Thank you. Inshore with you. Over it. Now, my beauty . . .'

The fisherman lifted out his fish and carried it up the shingle.

He turned to me. He was very hot and rather breathless. 'He's not a bad fish,' he said, 'Twelve or fourteen pounds. Not more.' He spoke in quiet appraisement. I am sure that if I had told him that he had been talking aloud to that same fish for the last ten minutes, he would not have believed me. I wonder, is it so with us all?

Coarse-fishing a Hundred Years Ago

The Sporting Magazines of a hundred years ago were not much interested in fishing. Although they found a little space for cock-fighting and for prize-fights of 100 rounds; although they published the rules of the MCC for cricket and single wicket, in which runs were called notches and a side was fined five notches if one of its players stopped a ball with his hat; although they mention that a golf club had recently been established in Manchester, that the usual form for the links was square with a hole at each corner and that the game was played with a leather ball stuffed with feathers; although they argued fiercely over the respective merits of flint locks and new-fangled percussion caps; they were completely dominated by the horse. Nothing else really mattered to them. In 1826 the horse ruled the world. Even the King was patted on the back for loyalty to the true monarch when he forbade the shooting of foxes on the royal estates. The drivers of the stage-coaches were of greater public interest than most Members of Parliament. We read of stage coachmen who had tailors' bills of £90 a year and drove in white kid gloves, wearing out a pair and tossing them away every dozen miles. We read detailed criticism of individual coachmen, like nothing in our day but 'Cricketer's' affectionate severities about members of the Lancashire team. The conductors on the coaches were of no more importance than policemen round the cricket field. One writer, indeed, complained of having to tip them even when 'they were not provided with fire-arms and were therefore no protection' against the hold-ups which occasionally occurred. Importance was for the horse and for him alone, though he reflected a little on those who actually handled him. Coaching, racing and fox-hunting were the things. Nimrod was an international celebrity. Pheasants were damned as England's ruin because those who preserved them became 'Vulpecides and Sons of Belial'. Fox-hunting saved England from the fate of Rome, by enabling men 'to dart like lightning across the country instead of leading lazy idle lives, crawling through the world like fat maggots, or dozing like fat aldermen by their own firesides and dying at last of sloth and inactivity.' Violent exercise and hard drinking then went together, and we read of a man who gulped three bottles of port at three successive draughts, but, on being offered a fourth, 'excused himself as he was going to several other parties and was afraid he might get a drop too much.'

It is surprising that fishing held up its head at all in these robust and noisy pages. But it is even more surprising that the kind of fishing which filched most space from the earnest debaters of grass versus oats and the comparative merits of coachmen on the northern and southern roads, was not salmon or trout fishing but the fishing which most fox-hunters nowadays are ready to leave to the working men's clubs. Among the engravings of celebrated horses there is one of two gentlemen wearing white trousers, and top hats, engaged in playing and netting a pike. The pike, we are told, weighed 8 pounds and its captor would like to ask a sporting friend 'What he thinks of a *plunge* that makes you jump again and then a *run* of twenty yards across the river? I know he will cry out in ecstasy, "The Devil take foxhunting"; though he don't mean it.' Then there is an engraving of a 9 pound carp 'taken by that excellent angler, Mr Chase of Arundel, on the 5th of May (!) in the river Arun, in the eddy so well known to anglers called the Crab Tree Hole' ... Two days later, we learn, Mr Chase took another, of $6\frac{1}{2}$ pound which 'being hooked on the outside of its mouth, was very formidable in the water.' There is a long correspondence on the catching of carp, in which some desperadoes even asked for instruction in the use of nets.

Coarse-fishing a Hundred Years Ago

I had never heard of fly-fishing for carp until I looked through these old magazines. But here are elaborate engravings of carp flies, remarkable for long fluff whisks, curled like sheeps' horns. Carp, generally, take up their fair share of space. There is even an account of one which sat so patiently for its portrait that it was honoured by presentation to the President of the Royal Academy. But the pike fishers became impatient. One, writing in February on the carp question, ejaculates in a post-script that 'A more beautiful season for fishing pike never was seen.' Another says that pike-fishing 'is as superior to carp-fishing as fox-hunting is to ferreting.' There are a few inter-esting side-lights on other methods of coarse fishing. We are advised to fish for dace with 'small compact flies' embellished with gentles, and we are given a recipe for a ground bait which might be worth trying today. A quarter of a pound of old Cheshire cheese, bruised in a mortar with the lees of olive oil to the consistency of a thick paste. To this add a pennyworth of rosewater, and divide it into little balls not bigger than a pea. 'Strew them in the water where you design to angle.'

All this, in a magazine otherwise almost exclusively occupied with horses and meant for readers for whom fox-hunting was the serious business of life, suggests that the curious caste feeling which even today leads some trout fishers to look down on other kinds of angling is a newer thing than one had thought and not an old tradition. There is other evidence of an even more convincing kind. We hear nothing of the price of salmon rivers, but these fox-hunters and drivers of four-in-hand are told of 'subscription waters with good pike and perch.' People who used the 'King's Arms' had a free range of some water on the Lee. Others paid 2s. 6d. a day. The principal fish were chub, roach, dace and gudgeon. Another water at a guinea a year is recommended because it contains 'very fine eels'.

What little there is about fishing for salmon and trout is interesting. As long ago as 1826 it was complained that 'the very nature of a thorough angler is almost obsolete – the steam engine has everywhere scared the lonely fisherman.' Even then people were complaining of the scarcity of fish and there was talk of pollution in the Usk. Let it be set down now to the credit of the men of Hereford (whose descendants have no doubt forgotten it) that for some time they refused to have their streets lit with gas 'on the plea that the pipes communicating with the river would destroy the fish' in the Wye. A tablet of gold should commemorate these worthy men. Their hearts at least were in the right place. Another reason than pollution is suggested for the shortage of trout in Brittany. It is put down to the strict keeping of Lent, 'for although the men have less religion than Hottentots, yet the women and old people have a double stock,' and everybody is made to eat fish or starve.

A Kettle of Fish

'A rare kettle of fish I have discovered at last,' said Squire Western. 'Who the devil would be plagued with a daughter?' There, already, a kettle of fish has its modern significance. But at that time real kettles of fish were still being boiled on the banks of the Tweed. That remarkable footman, John Macdonald, who introduced the umbrella into England, saw Sterne die, travelled widely, enjoyed 'the keen searching air' which he found at St Helena but preferred the view from the Castle of Stirling to any out of Scotland, describes very well the real kettles of fish that were known in the eighteenth century. 'The noblemen and gentlemen that have estates by the Tweed side, in the summer and harvest give what they call a kettle of fish. The entertainment is conducted in the following manner. They all have marquees for the purpose, which they pitch near the banks of the river. Orders are given for a large dinner, and plenty of wine and punch. The fishermen take the salmons out of the water and that moment cut them in pieces, throw them into boiling water, and when done, serve them up on table. This treat is called a "krab of fish." There is always music to play after dinner. Some of the company walk along the banks of the Tweed; others play at cards; and the younger part of the ladies and gentlemen dance country dances on the grass. They conclude with tea and syllabubs; and then go home.' Even the Oxford English Dictionary, though its notes both meanings of the phrase, does not explain how the name of this simple pastoral entertainment came to be applied to such troubles as those of Squire Western over his refractory daughter. Nowadays, 'pretty', 'nice' and 'fine' kettles of fish are common enough in the affairs of men, but are no longer boiled to the

accompaniment of music and dancing, wine, punch and syllabubs on the grassy banks of Tweed. The nearest thing to a
kettle of fish that is known today is the admirable *ukhá* or fish
soup boiled at the riverside by Russian fishermen. But that is
made with the kind of fish that is scorned by the cooks of
Scotland and England.

There are fashions in fish. It is possible in angling literature
to watch, for example, the decline and fall of the pike from the
eminence he once enjoyed. He was once for the angler 'my joy
of all the scaly shoal' and when cooked 'too good' for any but
those who fished for him 'or very honest men'. With the pike
the other coarse fish have lost their kitchen reputations. Yet
once upon a time a pike would be the chief dish at a banquet
and many another fish now seldom cooked was valued as highly
as trout or salmon. At the Assizes in Derby in 1613, the bill of
fare included '15 several sorts of fowl, among others young
swans, knots, herns, bitterns, etc., three venison pasties
appointed for every meal, 13 several sorts of sea-fish, 14
several sorts of freshwater fish, each appointed to be ordered a
different way . . .' Eleven of these several sorts must have been
fish without adipose fins. In the seventeenth century the lack of
an adipose fin in no way barred a fish from honour at the table.
Fish ponds were still being stocked, not for angling alone but
for food, with the same fish that fed the monks on Fridays and
in Lent. In 1674 Sir John Reresby stored two fish ponds at
Thryburgh near Rotherham with tench and carp. Fifty years
later Defoe observed a regular trade between the Fen country
and London 'for carrying fish alive by land carriage'. 'This
they do by carrying great buts fill'd with water in waggons, as
the carriers draw other goods: the buts have a little square flap,
instead of a bung, about ten, twelve, or fourteen inches square,
which, being open'd, gives air to the fish, and every night,
when they come to the inn, they draw off the water, and let
more and sweet water run into them again. In these carriages
they chiefly carry tench and pike, perch and eels, but especially

tench and pike, of which here are some of the largest in England.'

Seventy years later, coarse fish were honoured still. Mrs Elizabeth Raffald, who flourished towards the end of the century, was housekeeper to the Lady Elizabeth Warburton and subsequently kept a cook-shop in Manchester, crowned her life by the writing of a book called, *The Experienced English Housekeeper*, 'for the use and ease of Ladies, House-keepers, Cooks, etc., Written purely from Practice'. My copy of the great work, with as frontispiece a portrait of the author in a mob-cap, her eyes sparkling with demure pride in her profession, was printed by G. Bancks in Manchester, in 1798 (the same year as the *Lyrical Ballads*). Mrs Raffald (like Words-worth) had none of the modern contempt for coarse fish. She puts trout and perch together, with just a hint of a superior respect for perch. She describes a stew of carp and tench as 'a top-dish for a grand entertainment'.

With the development of our sea fisheries, of our means of transport and of the laziness of cooks, freshwater-fish other than trout and salmon fell out of favour. They are still prized abroad. In the markets of Russia may be seen huge tubs full of big perch and pike and other fish. The marketing housewife chooses her fish alive and so is assured of its freshness. Barges half full of water like vast floating bait-cans lie along the quays of the Neva and the fishermen use a long handled net to dip out their fish for their customers. Over vast areas of Russia the 'game' fish are unknown and the 'coarse' fish still enjoy the reputation which they had in eighteenth-century England. A cookery book in my possession, used by an officer's mess on the Russian front during the war, gives 23 ways of cooking pike, 8 ways of cooking carp and 12 ways of cooking tench. It offers 9 recipes for eels, 11 for bream, 8 for perch, 6 for trout and 7 for salmon. The pike-perch (*Lucioperca*), an excellent sporting fish, which has, I think, been introduced into England, is honoured by the description of 24 methods of cooking him.

These recipes do not include a number of different rissoles, vinaigrettes and mayonnaises of pike, tench, carp, and perch and special fish dishes for Lent. Nor do they include the fish soups, of which some well-thumbed pages give a score, to be made from carp, eel, tench, pike, perch, ruffe and burbot, besides sturgeon and other specially Russian fish. 'For the best soup,' authority tells us, 'there must be a pound of fish for each plateful of soup. For ordinary soup half that quantity suffices.'

In Russia to this day a kettle of fish (*ukhá*) is often the most important part of a banquet. Curiously enough the two fish chiefly prized for this purpose are two which are not often eaten in England, the ruffe and the burbot. *Ukhá* for a banquet is made by putting ruffes or perch (preferably ruffes) in a vessel of cold water and then thoroughly boiling it. Into this boiling stock are thrown choice bits of burbot and other fish. The liver of the burbot is particularly prized and there is a tradition that the poor burbot should be beaten before cooking, so that his liver may be enlarged, a practice analogous to that cruel whipping to death of sucking pigs which Lamb described as refining the violet. The whole brew is sometimes enlivened by the addition of wine. But the *ukhá* which corresponds most nearly to the Tweedside kettles of fish is made by parties of fishermen at the waterside. This *ukhá* is made from whatever fish are caught. Towards evening the camp fire is made on the bank and in a warm luminous hollow in the river mist the fishermen sit and burn their throats with fresh-made soup. If only one could be as sure of catching fish in England, who would carry sandwiches? Beside the fish nothing is needed but salt, pepper and an onion. A bait-can makes an admirable kettle.

Uncaught Fish

Some uncaught fish have an elasticity that deprives others of the respect and credibility that they deserve. While failing to catch roach the other day, I observed a young man, at the bend of the river below me, tugging and testing a cast and running, with almost frantic haste, his line through the rings of his rod. 'Broken me,' he shouted, 'gone off with float and pilot and twenty yards of line. Ten or twelve pounder at least.' A little later a farmer approached this young man to ask if he had leave to fish in that place. He had, and after he had satisfied the farmer, I heard him tell anew in a voice still high pitched by his excitement of the story of his loss. 'The fish was a fifteen-pounder if he was an ounce.' A little later I moved up river to fail to catch roach in another perfect hole, and was presently passed by a pike spinner. 'Anything doing?' he asked. 'There would be if I could fish,' I replied. 'There's a man in the field below,' he said, 'who has had a twenty-pounder on and lost him.' In the evening the young man was still fishing in the same place. My companion, whom, as he came by from fishing higher up, I had told of the adventure of the young man, went down to him. When he returned, he said, 'That fish has grown to twenty-five pounds.' Now there was a fish that had never been seen but had grown from ten to twenty-five pounds in the course of a short autumn fishing day. There are so many of these indiarubber fish that they reflect on the good faith of fish less expansive but with a greater claim to honour.

Your honest uncaught fish has quite different qualities. For one thing, he has been seen. He is not a myth, made to excuse a violent strike that would have broken the line with nothing but a two-pound jack at the end of it. Those who have seen him are scrupulously modest in their estimates of his size. They do not want to catch their whale and find him a minnow, and still less do they want such a humiliating operation to be performed for them by a friend. So, if anything, they underestimate him. But they have seen him. They know he is there to be caught. He is for them what the White House is said to be to American babies, a legitimate aim to stimulate ambition.

Not long ago I was looking through a friend's tackle and asked what was the purpose of a gigantic red-tipped spoon armed with a single vast triangle. 'Oh,' he said, 'that is for my big pike in the eddy where the Something flows into the Something Else. I go and offer it to him two or three times a year. Some day he'll take it.' Now that was an uncaught fish worthy of the name. My friend spoke of him as Captain Ahab spoke of Moby Dick. That fish shed glamour for him on the whole river. In York Street, Westminster, was a house that was tenanted once by Milton and later by William Hazlitt. That house was like an eddy that had held big ones. The Adelphi, until Mr George Bernard Shaw leaves it, holds a big one yet. While he is there, there is excitement in visiting even the least distinguished of his fellow-inhabitants, the bleak and gudgeon of that romantic place. So it is with the uncaught fish. When news comes that that big pike is no more every man who fishes the river will feel the loss of him, and most of all, no doubt, the man who catches him at last, if he deserves him and is not some interloper from elsewhere who does not know *whom* he has caught.

It is a happy dispensation that replaces one big one by another, Milton by Hazlitt. We can almost be sure that if in a certain pool we lay siege to a huge fish and at last catch him, we shall, sooner or later, be laying siege to another in the very same place. Among trout, particularly, the order of precedence is strict and ambition strong. Benefices are not left long without incumbents. It is as if each trout in the river knew each good place and its value in daily food. You catch the two-pounder

under the willow at the bend, eat him, and next day, behold, he has shrunk a little, it is true, but is rising under the willow as before. The juniors have all had a move up. William Caine has a delightful story of a man, home from China after seven years, going straight to the spot that he remembered and finding his monster at home. 'Ten days I fished for him, and I got him in the end. And here he is again for me. Oh! I like chalk-stream fishing.' And a little later: 'Three and a quarter. He's grown half a pound since I slaughtered him seven years ago.' In chalk streams this, or something like it, happens often. They are less variable than our northern rivers and their trout are less nomadic. In our waters it happens sometimes, but our trout are not so large, and seldom achieve fame until they cease to be uncaught fish.

Salmon and sea-trout can gain the dignity of uncaught fish only from flood to flood. They are visiting strangers, and prolonged intimacy with them is impossible. Nor can shoaling fish ever be counted among the great uncaught. You may say that in such and such a place *are* big roach, but not that there *is* a big roach. On the other hand, a man may see a big carp in a pond and be its slave for years. It is the singular number that makes your uncaught fish. Pike, I think, are the best of them. The pike grows to such a size. He has the strength and the cunning to accumulate a magnificent past of triumphs over those who have sought to catch him; rod tops smashed, lines broken, hooks straightened out, weedings innumerable. A great trout may survive a season or two, but there are pike with histories as long as that of the Trojan War, pike to have been broken by whom is a distinction.

When I hear of a great pike captured where no one expected him I feel that he is a wasted fish. Better far that twenty men should fail to catch him, so that he should glorify the river for us all. A man I know dropped two partridges with a right and left. One fell in the river. He marked where the other fell and turned to see nothing in the river but the subsiding ripples of a great commotion and his spaniel swimming round looking for the partridge that was no longer there. Next morning my friend brought the second partridge to the riverside, tied some big trebles in it and hove it into the air with his pike rod so that it splashed into the water just where the other had disappeared. It was gone on the instant, and my friend landed a twenty-five pounder. Now that was really good fishing, but waste of an uncaught fish. The fish should have been hooked and lost a time or two, should have been watched, cruising like a submarine, should have been seen chasing pound roach like minnows, should have defeated sundry friends invited to try for him, should have survived a year or so, and been caught at last to round off magnificently a rich chapter of my friend's life. As it was, he was an uncaught fish only from five of an afternoon till eight of the following morning, and much of that time my friend, who alone knew of him, must have been asleep.

Rods out of Use

There are a few precise fishermen who on the 1st of October, the trout season being over, send their rods to the makers to be revarnished and to have the whippings renewed. Some even leave their rods in store for better keeping, and receive them only a day or two before the season opens with an astonishing air of newness. Such men are like the amateur sailors who come to the waterside to find their sails already hoisted, the anchor short or the buoy rope ready to cast off, sail a race maybe, and then resign their boat to the professional. These sailors may be wonderful helmsmen, but they do not know the more intimate pleasures of owning a ship. And these fishermen may be wonderful artists when the rod is in their hands, but miss a great deal of the happiness of being a fisherman. There is something suspect, inhuman about them. They are very rare. Most fishermen do not like to be parted from their rods. If they do send them to be overhauled they are orphaned until they are returned and unhappy without them, even though it may be months before they can cast a line again. They more probably resolve to send them to the makers, but put off doing so and secretly rejoice to have them still hanging in their places. The happiest, of course, are those who can themselves do their own small repairs and know that some time during the winter they will have a good excuse for taking the rods from their cases. I am speaking, of course, of trout and salmon fishers, for the coarse fisher looks for some of the best of his sport in the winter months, when chub are at their best, when the weeds have gone, when you can spin a bait in the places that were impenetrable in summer and know that if that bait passes within reach of a pike fit for a glass case he is more likely to take it in winter than at any other time. It is not until March, when the trout fisherman is returning to the river, that the coarse fisher puts away his rods, and then only for three months, while the trout fisher, unless he fish for grayling, must wait a whole five.

He puts off for a month or two that first overhauling of his rods, just as during the hard time in Russia I used to put off, as long as I could bear my hunger, the single wretched meal that had to suffice for each day. And only when he can no longer leave the things alone he takes a rod down, opens the bag, takes out one joint and then another, and is without any intention of setting the rod up until he has actually done so and is feeling once more the magic touch of the familiar cork handle. A little unsatisfactory it is without the reel, so he puts that on too and wishes his ceilings were higher. More fine rod tips are smashed by the meanness of architects than at the waterside.

When he has taken out one rod the fisherman, unless he is very strong-minded, takes out another and compares it with the first (I do not refer to those grudging anglers who can afford motor-cars but think that one rod is enough). And the most curious things happen at this moment. A rod long ago laid aside in favour of what seemed to be a better and was certainly a newer reasserts its old dominion and becomes once more first favourite. Or, at greater expense, the fisherman is suddenly aware that the manifold errors of the last season, strikes too soon, too hard, or too late, splashes of flies that should have dropped like thistledown, were his rod's fault, not his own. And he gets out the tackle catalogues, reads ecstatic words by A, B, and C on the work of this or that maker, and on the morrow has made the first irrevocable step towards adding to his collection. It is a terribly easy thing to stop at Moult Street or the Market Place. Postcards, too, are written in a moment, and once written may as well be posted. And tackle-makers are always ready to send a rod on approval, knowing by long experience that the fisherman has seldom the heart to return it. His imagination rushes forward, and he has caught the fish of a lifetime almost as soon as the rod is in his hand. It looks different from his own. Perhaps just that difference was all that was needed in his fishing. Anyhow, it is impossible to part with a rod on which one has caught a fish, if only in imagination. But the acquisition of a new rod in winter is salt to a man already thirsty. For a rod, though paid for, is hardly owned until the fair velvet cork of its handle is darkened, and until it has caught fish not only in imagination, but in actuality. Once it has done that it has its place in a fisherman's life. Whatever happens to it then it can never be less than the flower or ribbon of an old romance. Until then it is a thing with an urgent claim upon its owner. And when the season opens he throws aside all human claims upon him with an easy conscience, knowing that first things come first and that he owes it to his rod to bring it alive by letting it catch its first fish.

After that it is a thing in itself with an independent memory fit to hang with others of experience. But not until; and for that very reason I do not myself much care about buying a new rod until I can take it straight from the shop to the water-side. There is real discomfort in the knowledge that a perfectly new rod is hanging with those others and sounding a raw, un-mellowed note among those organ pipes of fishing memory. Few organs have the secret of finer harmonies than steal from a row of rods, each in its case, graded carefully from the great salmon rod to the little many-jointed thing that has done much travelling in its day. There are some who are puffed up by wireless and listen to loudspeakers braying out programmes they have not chosen. More fortunate is the fisherman who, when he has put his rods away again, happily with no broken tips, can look along that row of drab twill cases and hear the ripple of the water, the cart-wheel splash of the monster, and see again the shadow under the trees, the sunlight on the stream, and flies floating down. This rod takes him to the Dove at Ilam, this after sea-trout in Scotland or on the Hodder, this belongs to the smooth chalk streams and water meadows of the south, this to the swifter, more boisterous waters of the north. They sound together an incomparable symphony.

Chub

Towards the end of last week there seemed to be some promise of better weather for grayling fishing, and I took down a rod for the first time this year and went off to a grayling river with a good supply of cockspurs and brandlings. Several other people had made the same mistakes, and there was a decided melancholy in the inn. The river was still full. It dropped a little one day, but rain in the night brought it up again, and on Friday it was rising all day. On Saturday the last of the other fishermen departed. He had caught in three days' fishing one sizable fish, but on the last day, he said, he had had hold of something big, which had broken away from him. He thought it must have been a chub. Until he said this I had forgotten that there were chub in the river. There are not a great many, but in some stretches they are to be found, just as in some stretches there are a few pike. It is not a regular chub river like the Wyre and no one visits it with the special object of fishing for chub. Chub, in fact, in the north, do not get the attention they deserve. In the Wyre, for example, people complain that the chub are so many and so rapacious that on some days they will not allow sea-trout to take a fly, grabbing it themselves before the sea-trout have a chance at it. One would think that in winter the trout fishers, anxious to improve the river, would spend a little time in fishing for chub, just as in other rivers they fish in winter for grayling and pike, thus having their cake and eating it, getting good winter fishing and thereby making summer and autumn fishing better.

Now this disappointed grayling fisher spoke of that chub with contempt instead of gratitude, though the chub had given the only moment of interest to a melancholy day. On such a day I should feel ready to forgive a chub (who should take my bait) his presence in a river normally without need of him, since it has salmon and trout for the warmer months and grayling for the months in which we cannot fish for these. I felt that he was a little ungrateful to that chub, and thought how odd it was that in different parts of the country the same fish should be so differently esteemed. I remembered the last occasion on which I had heard a man speak of chub, in the evening of a day made memorable for me by a Thames trout.

There is in the south country an inn of a most pleasing character with a delightful name. It is called The Rose Revived, and its signboard, painted by a celebrated architect, shows a rose being revived in a glass of sherry. This inn is hard by a bridge called New Bridge, because it is the oldest over the Thames. To this inn in the evening many fishermen gathered from the roach-swims up and down the river; and in the moonlight outside it I met an old man for whom, without knowing him, I felt already some affection, since he was a living witness that on that day I had caught the biggest trout I had ever caught and, for a simple reason, had not got that trout to gloat over or to eat or to put into a glass case. He was, though a mere human being, a representative, as it were, of that very handsome, happily departed fish. He had been on the opposite bank of the river, and had watched me land this big and wise Thames trout who, knowing that the season was just over, had risked himself on my roach tackle. It had taken me a long time to cozen him out from under the willow branches draped with weed by the late floods, and when I had carefully weighed him (3 pounds, 4 ounces and a little bit over) all the bystanders breathed heavily as I slid him into the water again. The old man whom I met in the moonlight by the inn had left his own fishing to watch the episode I have just set down; and now, as if to comfort me for being without my noble trout, he offered me a box of stewed wheat with which, he said, I should catch gigantic roach. And then he began to talk of the river the

Thames had been, and how the passion of his life was neither
for trout nor roach (though he had not a word to say against
these fish) but for chub. He told me that he had fished for chub
for thirty-five years, and always had set them back for the good
of the river, even as I had set back my Thames trout. In the
north a captured chub has a better chance of being thrown over
a hedge than of being returned to the water, in which he is
considered vermin and nothing more. Yet, like Goldsmith, he
can say that there are places where he, too, is admired. Many
years ago an old fisherman, about to die, knowing that he
could fish no more, made me a present of his chub-float, a
monstrous thing of cork and quill, and, as he gave it me, told
me of this or that old loggerhead who had dragged it under
water. It was almost as if he were the dying priest of some
heathen religion presenting me on his death-bed with the sacri-
ficial knife, exulting in retrospect on the victims who had felt
it. In the moonlight by that old bridge over the Thames, I
remembered this old float and its long-dead owner; and
listening to the enthusiasm of the old chub-hunter I thought
how strange a passion this is that singles out here a man and
there a man and makes of him a fisherman apart, to pursue
this nervous, handsome, altogether uneatable fish. I remembered J. W. Martin's story of Chubber Childs, who, after they
had been separated many years, sent Martin a message to say
'that he was after them yet', knowing that Martin would know
exactly what he meant. And then the old chub-hunter began
to speak of baits for chub, of which there are no end, and he
praised exceedingly the tail of the cray-fish, in this way re-
minding me of Aksakov and of sunlit days on the Moscow
river, and of fishing of the kind Aksakov loved. Aksakov is full
of praise of the cray-fish as a bait for chub and some of his
equally rapacious cousins. The old man went on to tell me a
strange thing. With the tail of a cray-fish, he said, he could
catch great quantities of chub, but when he could not get that
bait and bought prawns or dug lobworms, or shaped lumps of

paste, or sank his hook in a cherry, he could catch him never a chub, though with these baits other men were successful who could do nothing with his cray-fish. And all the time as he spoke of the chub there was a warm glow in his words, that sort of glow that is in the words of some men when they speak of salmon, the sort of passion that I have felt in a bear hunter describing the tracking of the bear. And now, up here in the north, there was this grayling fisher talking of the hooking of that chub with as much contempt as if he had got hold of an old bucket.

The Coldest Day

Monday and Tuesday of this week were not the days on which one would normally choose to go fishing. In retrospect, illumined by the limelight of the newspapers, they seem even worse than they were. A tidal harbour was frozen up, swans were frozen to death in the ice, waterfalls were immobile cascades of glass, the main street of Appleby was used for tobogganing, a purpose for which it is particularly fitted, and the only way of getting out of one's waders at night was to thaw them before the kitchen fire of the Tufton Arms. Even the fishable area of the river was lessened by broad belts of ice, and this not that cat ice at the edges which the grayling fisher welcomes as the promise of a good day, but ice that would in many cases bear the fisherman, who had to get into the stream above it and wade gingerly along its edge, watching carefully lest it should push him into water deeper than his wading stockings. Still, it was such an opportunity as might not offer again of seeing whether there is any weather too hard for the grayling. Pritt and Walbran, those two great Yorkshiremen, couple frost and grayling together. Pritt speaks of grayling taking with the thermometer at 18 deg. (before and after noon it stood somewhere near this on Monday), and says, rightly, that a struggle with a good fish 'is any time as good as a sudden rise of 20 degrees. No amount of cold,' he says, 'will prevent the fish coming at your worm.' Walbran does not go quite so far, but he does say that for many years he made a point of taking six consecutive days after grayling in the week following Christmas (our noses are closer to the grindstone now), and he speaks of days when much time had to be wasted in clearing the ice from the line. Monday, with a hard frost and a

173

sprinkling of snow in the morning, was a clear invitation to the game, and just after eleven we were walking through the sparkling fields.

We found that the cold was by no means too great for the grayling, but did very greatly increase the difficulties of the grayling fisher. The most important quality of a worm swum for grayling, is the same as that of good manners – a simplicity and naturalness that shall at least seem unaffected. The grayling can use both his eyes and his brains. 'The gimlet eyes of a mother-in-law,' says Pritt, are less piercing than his, and in this very low clear water there is nothing to prevent him from using them. He is suspicious of any movement, and the fisherman can frighten him off at least as easily as he can scare a summer trout. The broad ice edging of the river acts as a sounding-board in repeating and multiplying ripples. That is bad enough, but the really serious difficulty in such a frost as that of Monday is to preserve the naturalness of the worm swimming down the stream. It should move at precisely the same pace as the water. It should not move erratically, varying its progress down-stream with staccato jerks in the opposite direction. But, when the line becomes a necklace of glass beads and the rings of the rod are blocked by little studs of ice, this is precisely what happens. I had hoped that the big rings of my new rod would have counteracted this, but, though they did prevent the line from freezing to the rod, they did not, for more than a cast or two after each thawing, allow the line free passage. The worst was the agate end-ring, partly because, being at the end, it collected most water and partly because it was much too small. The others were still free long after it had frozen solid. Still, both my friend and I did catch grayling.

On the Tuesday we were cheered to our fishing with the news that the Eden was frozen from one side to the other at Appleby. The cold was slightly less intense, but there was a hard wind which made it seem much worse. The ice-belts on the edge of the river were wider and thicker, and I began fishing without much hope, but determined, if it could be done, to find a way of dealing with that problem of the freezing line and rings. The wind — that very wind which made my head feel as if it had been trepanned — showed me the way. I made the wind my master, as if, instead of standing thigh-deep in the freezing Eden, I was dapping the Mayfly in hot June sunshine. Using the finest, lightest line I had (Illingworth 4x), I used the wind to keep the whole of it clear of the water, and ended the day with my rod still dry and not a single drop of water frozen in the rings. I was rewarded by a respectable but not a large basket of grayling, of as high an average size as any I have had from this admirable water. But it is one thing to strike a grayling with a long line on the water and quite another to strike him with line as fine as this in the air, going straight from rod-tip to float, with the fish only eighteen inches below it. The slightest movement is sufficient, and, accustomed to the other way, I lost two casts in fish. I also lost a rather high percentage of fish after hooking them, but that is to the credit of the grayling. One, in particular, was a very good one who leapt three times from the water, then made a long run across the river, turned suddenly, and was gone. No one, I may say, has a right to throw a stone at the grayling for his alleged meek spirit who has not fished for him in Christmas week. He fights in a different manner from that of a trout, but not less hard. My landing-net got wet, naturally, and turned into a glass bucket, very beautiful to look at but useless for landing fish. It had to be thawed sufficiently for use by holding it under water. On one occasion I had to keep a fish waiting for it in clear, smooth water, close to me. The essential difference between his play and that of a trout seems to be that, while the trout dashes here and there, the grayling, hanging himself on your line, tries to swim backwards with rapid, flailing sweeps of his big tail and long body. It is this, I think, that has made people say that he tries to hit your line with his tail. While he thus violently 'backs water' he may indeed touch the gut with his tail, in which case you lose him, but I doubt whether he hits the gut of set purpose. But if he gets into a strong stream and below you this trick of his makes him seem twice as heavy as a trout of the same weight, and it is, I think, this, rather than any softness in the mouth, that, accounts for the large proportion of grayling hooked and lost. On Tuesday the best way of dealing with the smaller fish (half-pounders: we had none less) was to 'beach' them on the ice. If the landing-net was to be used it had to be kept in the river. It was the same with our waders. Flexible enough when wading in the stream, they turned to stiff glass tubes the moment we came out on the bank. That part of my line which the fish pulled under water turned to a stiff glass pencil when it was again in the air. The river was the warmest place to be in, and, what with those admirable grayling and the Pennines, whose peaks on Monday showed rose in the sunset above the snow mist that hid their massive bulk, I am come to think that those are feeble-minded who think it necessary to go to Switzerland for winter sport.

Left-handed Winding

It seems that there are fishermen who regard left-handed winding as a heresy, unsound in theory and almost monstrous in practice. Let me discuss it in detail. Another good day on the Eden, when the grayling came as freely as if they were themselves interested in the testing of left-handed reels, has left me even more firmly convinced that for winter grayling fishing at least right-handed winding is a handicap. If it is a handicap in grayling fishing it is hardly likely to be an advantage in any other kind, though in grayling-fishing, with a free-running reel fixed above the hand there are a few additional points to be made in favour of winding with the left hand. Consider for a moment what happens when, either float or fly-fishing, we cast, hook and land a fish with a single-handed rod. With a double-handed rod, there may be more to be said for the old method.

In the ordinary way the fisherman has his reel below the handle of his rod, with its handles on the right side. He casts with the rod in his right hand. He is still holding it so when he hooks his fish. Having hooked the fish at some considerable distance he needs to bring it towards him but finds that he cannot get at the reel with his left hand and is consequently powerless until he has transferred the rod from the right hand to the left. This change of hands is made almost immediately after the strike and it is not surprising that the first lesson that the beginner has to learn is, to keep a taut line while making it. A few fish lost at that precise moment are usually enough to teach him. But it seems to me that they might just as well have taught him to avoid making that change at all. He then plays the fish with the rod in the less sensitive, comparatively dead

177

hand. The delicate antenna of the rod reports the actions of the fish to the left instead of to the right hand, that is to say, to the inferior receiving instrument of the two. If all goes well the fish is presently within reach of the net. Now the net hangs usually on the fisherman's left side, attached to the fishing bag, which is so placed as to leave the right arm free. Either he has to fumble for it across himself (round himself in the case of elderly and well-built fishermen) or he has again to change hands, taking the rod in his right while he gets the net in his left. If the fish comes in easily, he may net it so. But if, as often happens, it makes a last dash and takes off line again, he had to make yet another change of hands in order to wind that line in again, this time gripping the net under his arm as he does so. Then, if all goes well, he has the net in his right hand and the rod in his left. This may be preferable, but every fisherman has landed fish both ways. What does seem to be deplorable is the number of changes from one hand to the other during the tussle. Perhaps, in the case of large fish, which have to be gaffed or tailed, it is better to have the rod in the left hand. But for playing even these the right hand is better. Now if the reel is so arranged that the handles are on the left all the earlier and more dangerous changes of hand are eliminated and we are left with a single change, at the end, and that only in landing fish too big to go into the net.

Right-handed winding was probably adopted when reels were clumsy, stiff and awkward, like the old winches, needing some coaxing before they would do their work. It persists today when reels are much more efficient than most fishermen. It has persisted through so many generations of fishermen that left-handed winding seems, when it is first tried, almost against nature. It was, I think, the Illingworth reel that broke this ancient barrier of prejudice and tradition. That reel cannot be wound except with the left hand and there were those who objected to it on that account, not realizing that this was one of its advantages. In single-handed spinning, left-handed winding is more important than in any other kind of fishing. The moment in which a cast is spoil for fishing purposes is the moment in which the bait enters the water. The fishermen must get it immediately on the move and, using the old method, he has to change the rod from one hand to the other before he can begin winding in. He can get the minnow on the move by throwing up the rod end in the moment of changing hands, but this leaves the rod in the wrong position, too high. I got into the way of doing this with a little American multiplier, with the Malloch and with the Silex. With the Malloch it is possible to change hands while the bait is flying out. It was the Illingworth that proved that this difficulty was not one to be met by skill in juggling and that it was nothing but the old familiar difficulty of breaking an established tradition. If you wind with the left hand that difficulty does not need to be met, because it does not exist. A single day's fishing in this way is enough to make the fisherman wonder at his own conservatism.

It remains, of course, to make ourselves complete nuisances to the fishing-tackle makers, who are, if possible, more conservative than fishermen and with better reason. They dislike making spinning minnows in pairs, to spin opposite ways, for the reason that this adds to the cost of manufacture. They will, at first, dislike still more the small changes in their business that the growing use of left-handed reels will occasion. Fly-reels, for example, are set below the hand, in order the better to balance the rod. If we simply reverse the reel, for left-handed winding, the line must run out from the uppermost side of the reel possibly cutting the fingers in the case of a prolonged run, unless we persuade the makers to reverse the usual gradation of the check springs, so that the check is hard against the fish and a mere velvet purr when the angler is winding in. Those delightful luxuries in precious stone, the agate lineguards on the more expensive reels, will have to be fitted on the other side. Most fly-wheels, however, are so built that the line cannot play truant, even without the agate ring. With reels for coarse fishing the lineguard question is more serious. Some men can fish without one, but, with a fine line, it is uncommonly easy to catch it round the handles of the reel or round the reel itself. I think we must persuade the tackle-makers to supply reels with the lineguard so fixed as to be in front when the reel handles are on the left. If they will make these little changes, they will, in the end, profit by making all other reels old-fashioned. Until they do them, we must manage as best we can, but, once we have tried it, we shall fish with our reel handles on the left, though by doing so we turn the best of their reels into makeshifts.

Changing the Weather

Of course there is plenty of weather that we should not wish to change. Who would wish to alter an early summer day, with an up-stream wind over water of the right height, sunshine, but not too much of it, and a happy absence of mist? Nor would any wise man seek to change a perfect day for winter grayling fishing (and this season, though things look black at the moment we have had plenty of them), steady sunshine, a clear water, frost morning and evening but, from the time we come to the river until the gathering dusk sends us home for tea, a crisp air, just not cold enough to freeze the drops of water on the line. The days that need improvement are not even those of moderate promise, which may easily be changed for the worse. There are, however, days when any change would be for the better, days when, if we had not come a long way to the river and if we did not know that we must be back at work tomorrow, we should leave our rods in their cases and declare that fishing was impossible. The fisherman who lives on the banks of a stream and can fish whenever weather and water combine to suit him, can leave such days alone. But most of us travel a long way to our water, and though the barometer and the weather report may have encouraged us at starting, it happens only too often that we move from one climate to another in crossing a range of hills and, on coming to our fishing, find that we have chosen a day on which we might just as well have stayed at home.

On such days, if we must fish and want to avoid an empty basket, resignation is a useless virtue. We must grasp our misfortune like a nettle. Half-hearted, hopeless, mechanical, resentful fishing is not fishing at all but waste of time, besides being very bad for the character. There is only one thing to do and that is to take the matter in our own hands and change the weather. And this is how we do it. We begin by looking the weather and the water squarely in the face and deciding exactly in what way the weather makes the fishing impossible. We cannot change the whole day or the whole river, but we can be clear in our own minds as to what is the particular effect of weather on river that makes it next door to hopeless to think of catching fish. Once we have decided what is the Greatest Common Unfavourable Factor we are a long way towards recovering interest in an otherwise discouraging day. We look at the river with new eyes, examining it for the places where that GCUF is least effective. On most kinds of bad day, the fish will seem to have been doing the same. By looking for and fishing in those places only we have, as fishermen, changed the weather for ourselves.

Snow-broth[1] and floating and submerged moving ice put grayling entirely off their feed. No man who lives by a grayling river would think of fishing for them under these conditions. But one day last week I had travelled a long way to come to a good reach of a river from which as a rule I can count on a decent basket (four to eight brace of fish). It was a clear, bright day, but, somewhere up in the hills there must have been a heavy snowfall and perhaps big drifts of snow into the river. Wading through the shallows was like wading through some fungus that had grown suddenly on the river bed. This was half melted snow on the bottom under the rising water. Masses of disintegrating snow were floating down. As far as one could see, up stream and down, were small flotillas of minute ice-bergs and the quieter water was mottled with thin moving patches on the point of freezing or thawing. Some of the pools were blocked from side to side with ice and snow. It was bad enough that the river had risen, making the finding of the fish

[1] By which I do not mean the water that comes from melted snow, but the real snow porridge described in this paragraph.

much more uncertain, but it was quite clear that the GCUF was not the water but the snow it carried with it. With the object of changing the weather I did more walking than fishing, and was rewarded by finding four places where for considerable periods there was no sign of floating snow or ice, these mischief-makers being held up or made to follow the rules of 'one way traffic', leaving a clean lane for my float, because of some beneficent conformation of rock or block of sludge on the shallows above them. In each of these four places the GCUF did not work. In each of them the weather, from the fisherman's point of view, was not that of this lamentable day. In each of them I had one offer from a grayling. One I missed. One I lost after a minute's play. Two I brought home in my basket. Two is not a crowd. But there is no need to explain to any fisherman that the difference between a basket with a brace of fish in it and a basket containing none at all is an absolute, not a relative difference. Eight and ten brace of fish may be about the same thing, but between two fish and nothing no sort of comparison is possible.

This principle of weather-changing, consciously or unconsciously, is applied in many ways. When wind, for example, is the GCUF it is instinctive. On a day when a hurricane roars down from the fells, without thinking twice about it, we change the windy day for one less windy, by seeking the sheltered stretches of the river. On a sultry day on a lake in summer we pursue, for a similar reason, every catspaw that ruffles the water. In a flood, we contradict the rush of water that tells us fishing is impossible, by finding our fish in the quiet eddies at the side. By this morning's post comes an example. A friend, seeking during the winter to do good to his trout stream, found it in high spate. But below a mill there were 150 yards of slack water and from this stretch in a couple of hours, he landed ten pike, spinning for them with a single-handed rod and a preserved gudgeon. He had eliminated the GCUF by fishing where it was inoperative.

We proceed in the same way when the GCUF has nothing to do with the weather. The worst of all fishing days, for me, are the days when someone is looking on. On such days I fish desperately, abominably and unhappily. There is no doubt at all in my mind as to the identity of the GCUF. The beast may even carry binoculars. My only hope is to give him the slip, to cross the river where he cannot follow, to run through a wood at risk of my rod, to double back under cover of a wall and, if these expedients fail, to turn regretfully to insult if no other means will change the weather for me by sending the GCUF off in dudgeon to spoil the fishing for someone else.

Wet and Dry Knowledge

Some days ago, when after grayling on a stretch of water that I had not fished before, I found myself wasting a good pool. I had made one or two assumptions about that pool that were quite unjustified. It had a deceptive because only superficial likeness to a pool in another river that I happened to know very well. As a result I started to fish it at the wrong place and so scared grayling instead of catching them. As I moved off with only half or less than half the grayling I ought to have taken from that pool, I knew that I had failed and badly failed to meet the true test of a fisherman, which is, that he shall be able to catch his share of fish in water that he is fishing for the first time. This is a very much harder test than that he shall catch double his share of his fish in water that he knows intimately. Indeed it is possible for intimate knowledge of one water to handicap a fisherman in fishing a different river, if it is knowledge that depends on other things than the look of the actual water.

Several of my friends have a thorough working knowledge of a particular stretch of a particular river. The moment they reach the riverside they look for certain marks, for example a shingle bed and a white boulder at the head of a stream. If the bank is bare they will not waste a moment in fishing the whole of a length of water that is always tempting in appearance and, if the river is a little up, is very good indeed. If the bank is covered, they will go straight to this length, confident that they will do well to start the day there. If the bank is covered at all deeply they know well that that length is as useless as if the river were too low. Again, the height of water on the white boulder tells them whether or not there is enough current in a short overflow stream to tempt the fish into it. If there is, they will cross to the island, get to the head of the side stream, fish immediately above and below an overhanging willow and count the grayling that they know to be there as already half-way into their baskets. If the white boulder is covered altogether, they know that this side-stream is not worth fishing, as it becomes a violent sluice with insufficient shelter. Again, the appearance of the white boulder tells them whether to expect fish in the run above it or on the gravel shallow not far below. By long experience, they know the pools that look good and are worthless, the pools that keep visitors fishing half the day for an empty basket and the places that look worthless but are usually good for a fish. Yet not all of these men are first-class fishermen, because all the knowledge that I have just described is the knowledge of experience or tradition on a single river, and not knowledge applicable everywhere. It is topographical knowledge, dry rather than wet, depending on the appearance of stones, banks, trees and even ruder marks such as bridges or water-gauges.

It is knowledge worth having, too, much better worth having than the still more rudimentary learning of the man who thinks he knows a water because he has been told, has found by experiment and has remembered the 'smittal' places in it, at which he may, with the river at normal height, expect to find a fish. The keeper has told him that Long Pool is a good place. He has tried it and found it so. He knows that Viaduct Pool is poor, except at its lower end. The Stepping Stones mark another of the sources expected to contribute to his basket. All this sort of knowledge, useful as it sometimes is, might be set down in a guide to a fishery. It does not need a good fisherman to learn it like a parrot. With its help, even a bad fisherman is able to give a good account of himself – on his own river. Some local anglers earn their baskets and their reputations on this sort of knowledge alone. It is often said that local anglers pick their days and owe to this their high average of success. When

Wet and Dry Knowledge

I hear too much of this picking of days, I suspect that the local angler is not so good a fisherman as his fishing diary would suggest. I suspect that he depends too much on this kind of knowledge and that he is thrown out if the river varies a little. At its best height he knows that fish are to be caught in certain places. When it is higher or lower, he does not know where to find them. This is like knowing that one and two make three but being unable to deduce that two and four make six. On the other hand, there are local anglers who know their own streams so well that they are not at a loss on any stream. They know them with a different kind of knowledge and one far more difficult to acquire. They have learnt when fishing to read the water, not the banks.

There are more of such anglers in the north and west than on the famous southern rivers. The reason for this is the same as the reason why our fishing is so much less consistent than that of the chalk streams. It is not that there is greater variety of rivers, but that there is greater variety in each river. The typical south-country trout stream is so controlled by hatches and drains that its depth varies by inches when the depth of northern rivers vary by feet. The fish in the south-country stream are to be found in the same places day after day. The south-country fisherman looks carefully at the surface of the water, not to judge where he may find a fish but to know what effect the surface current will have on his cast when he has thrown his fly to a fish whose presence is easily perceived. For him, topographical, dry knowledge is enough and good throughout the season, so far as looking for fish is concerned. You may hear a south-country fisherman tell another that the trout, *the* trout, by the fourth clump of thistles on the left bank below the footbridge is today taking Pale Wateries. That is not the sort of information that is much good on Wharfe or Eden, Ribble or Lune. The north-country fisherman cannot go to the river day after day to make the same casts over the same places. If he fishes throughout a season he has fished a hundred different rivers without ever leaving his own. Every spate may alter the underwater condition of a pool. Nor do his fish so often help him by showing themselves. He is forced to rely on the study of the water itself to gain what in time comes to seem an instinctive knowledge of what is going on underneath it. It is on this 'wet' knowledge that he must depend when he goes to a strange river. His topographical, 'dry' knowledge is useful enough at home. Misfortune comes, as it came to me, when he applies the wrong kind of knowledge to a river he does not know. And the temptation is great, when he finds himself beside a pool which, but for the railway ticket in his pocket, he might mistake for a particular pool on another river that he has fished a hundred times. He goes straight to the familiar spot, and finds too late that it is not that spot but another.

English and American
Catalogues of Tackle

If emotion remembered in tranquillity is poetry, the reading
of tackle catalogues in winter must be something very like it.
Better than books on fishing they transport their readers to
the waterside. It is true that the purity of the poetry is sometimes marred by a base ingredient, a clutching at the pocket-
book on reading the prices of some of the tackle; but to allow
this to spoil the pleasure for more than a moment is to be one
with the critic who could not enjoy pictures of the nymphs and
shepherds of Arcady for asking 'What of the wasps?' There
are no wasps in Arcady and the man who knows how to read
fishing tackle catalogues has taught his eyes to blink at the
right places so that he does not see the prices. Enough for him
to see a picture of his favourite rod or of the one that would be
his favourite, if he had it. He exults, quite selflessly, in the
ingenuities of a new reel, but remembers how well he can do
with his own. The plates of flies send his mind skimming week
by week through the season. If he be a pike fisherman the
pictures of the newest spinners are enough to let him feel the
knock as the pike takes hold and he wonders whether the casts
he uses are strong enough to hold it or whether he would do
better with these neat boughten ones. Then there are the
creels he will never possess. How seldom has he been able to
fill his own. And folding landing-nets, against each one of
which he must defend the net that hangs upon his study wall.
And in all this defence of what he has there is a secret, pleasant
knowledge that here or there he will be overborne. Somewhere
his dialectic will be no match for that of the tackle-maker. His
is a losing game and, if he prolong deliciously the debate, it is
with the knowledge that the game will be well lost and he the

189

gainer by its losing. With this or that new bit of tackle, on such and such a water ... with that or this on such another ... not Stewart in all his glory will be his superior.

Then too, English fishing tackle catalogues share with novels and advertisements of patent medicines the power to give their readers a feeling of amazing intimacy with people they have never seen. People who buy a patent medicine seem to write jubilantly of their disgusting symptoms and happy cures. A great host of fishermen (whose enthusiasm perhaps meets barren ground at home) seem to use the catalogues to pour out their rejoicings in their purchases. They use them as some men use the correspondence columns of newspapers but, like the sundial, they register only the happy hours. No disappoint-ments or complaints are here, and the artless gratitude of men who have bought fishing tackle and are pleased with it rises in full-throated and harmonious choir. It would seem that no man catches a salmon when fishing for trout without writing to half the tackle-makers bidding them share his joy as the capture was made on this one's gut cast, that one's line, an-other's minnow tackle and a fourth's dainty rod which 'when the fight was over was straight as ever.' These letters lead one to marvel at the modesty of the tackle-makers. All their rods catch fish bigger than the biggest for which they were intended. Trout lines hold whales and iron-jawed sharks masticate in vain the delicate filament that its maker advertised as fit for roach. Some of the letters are distasteful compliments paid by the authors to their own skill. ... 'I struck ... played him for an hour and a half and landed him without a gaff ... a fine test of your tackle.' But most are as natural as bird song.

I was shocked to find nothing of the kind in the catalogue of a well-known American maker. The letters of American anglers are perhaps unprintable or unwanted for their place was taken by a comic article on fishing in general by an author who recommended a creel of his own to fit in the waistcoat pocket, guaranteed to hold all the fish that the purchaser would catch in a season. Apart from this misplaced frivolity, the American catalogue is to an English one what one of Lamb's 'books that are no books' is to a piece of literature. It is, however, interesting in another way, illustrating as it does the general difference between English and American fishing. Not that the fish are so very different. The difference is one of style, the difference between the long sentences of Burke and the abrupt cut and thrust of Hazlitt. America is the country of the short rod. We have seen rods grow shorter in England but not to this extent and I think they have reached their shortest and tend to grow longer again. To judge from this catalogue most American fishing is done by spinning from a canoe. For such fishing a six-foot rod is well enough: indeed, its only disadvantage is that its owner must depend more on reel than on rod for keeping a fish under control. This, I think, must be the reason why spinning reels in America are almost invariably multipliers. American rods are so short that the raising of the point makes very little difference to the length of the line. The angler must shorten the line itself, and be able to do this in a hurry.

Even in fly-fishing the Americans use shorter rods than ours. Thirteen or fourteen feet is the usual length for a salmon rod, and for dry-fly salmon fishing there is a rod of only ten feet. In the matter of spinners and 'lures' there seems to be an even greater variety in America than here. Besides the astonishing family of floating and diving wooden 'plugs' that have been introduced recently to the pike on this side, there are 'feather minnows', 'Trout Terrors', any number of gaudy flies with spinners at the head of them, 'Mississippi Bass Bugs', 'Shimmy Wigglers', 'Little Egypt Wigglers' (developments of the old bait of a bit of pork rind) and scores of others the users of some of which would be excommunicated with bell, book and candle by some of our more sensitive clubs. Consider, for example, the 'Devil Bug', 'made of hair from off the body of a deer'. 'The hair being porous makes the Devil Bug a dry fly and a most perfect bug for casting. When the fish strikes it the hair squashes like a live bug, which is so real to him that he tries to swallow it at once and when you land him the bug is all in his mouth.' And they call that thing a dry fly.

Fly-tying in Winter

No doubt the proper place for tying flies is at the waterside and the proper time is just before fishing, when, after seeing what fly is on the water, the perfect fisherman takes out his dubbing bag and ties one like it, 'and if he hit to make his fly right, and have the luck to hit also where there is store of trouts, a dark day, and a right wind, he will catch such store of them as will encourage him to grow more and more in love with the art of fly-making.' But perfection is hard to come by, and exact knowledge of flies and the assiduity of professional fly-tyers have made it less urgently desirable than it used to be, at least in this matter. Your fisherman is not very likely to find the trout feeding on a fly which has not got its place in every tackle-maker's catalogue. He wastes no time in tying one for himself, but takes one ready from his box and with it, let us hope, catches such store of trouts as will encourage him to buy more flies at the same shop.

Though the proper time for fly-tying may be the moment before fishing, the time when this art is likely to yield the greatest pleasure is out of the trout season altogether, when the disconsolate trout-fisher knows that another two months or so must pass before he may even try to catch a trout. Then fly-tying is the next best thing to fishing; it is the sort of licking of the lips that eases a thirsty man in a desert. You may renew the whipping on your rod, take your reels to pieces and oil them and put them together again, varnish the ring of your landing-net (a thing often left undone until it is too late), strip your line and air it; you may do all these things, but not one of them will bring you so near to fishing as the looking through of the scraps of fur and feathers that are meant for fishes'

193

mouths. And though it is decidedly good to go through your fly-boxes, it is not so good as to make new flies. A lover cannot for more than a moment or two contemplate a lock of his mistress's hair, but he can happily spend a deal of time in carving a table for her. Inspection cannot be prolonged without uncomfortable idleness. There is a limit to the number of times you can rearrange a fly-box without finding yourself out.

But in winter it is dark early. We must tie flies by artificial light, and this is likely to yield strange results if we do not pick out our silks and feathers beforehand, by day. Nor, since we can get no models, is winter the time to experiment in new dressings. We must make flies like those we have already tried and of patterns that we know will be useful. We can do, for example, with a dozen of Greenwell's Glory, and this, with its starling wing, dull-waxed yellow silk, gold thread, and coch-y-bondhu hackle, is a fly about which we are not likely to make mistakes, even by the light of a candle. Black spiders, too: there is always sense in filling up our stock of them, with red, black, orange, or orange and gold bodies, hackled with plain black cock's hackles or, better, the soft metallic blue-black hackles from the head and neck of a cock pheasant. A neighbour sent me the best feathered cock pheasant I have had for many years, and ever since, in spare moments after dark, I have been turning out the flies that I know I shall need during next season, pheasant tail and hare's ear (a good variety of stone-fly) and spiders of all kinds. J. W. Dunne's series of dry flies can be made in artificial light by a man who has seen no models if he has bought the materials, which are all described and sold by letters and numbers. 'Silk, blended M. and L.; Hackle, so many turns of J.12.' But the mathematical precision of such a recipe detracts from the pleasure of the cook. Something should be left to chance and taste and for winter tying I prefer old simple dressings; 'badger hackle, pheasant wings, and mallard whisks' – with such a recipe the cook has a latitude wholly desirable. The other way is like counting the plums that are to go into a pudding.

Too much precision catches at the mind just when it should be free for distant flights far from the circle of light in which, indoors, in winter, after dark, the fingers are shaping wings, twisting hackles, spinning the down of a hare's ear on a thread of lightly, wetly varnished silk. As you tie a fly you are already fishing it, and, while your fingers are busy under the lamp, it is only the Grand Vizier of your mind who superintends them. The Caliph, you, has moved in time and space. A summer stream laps about your knees, there is a noise of water in your ears, flies are hatching and floating down before your eyes, and there, just where the ripple turns to smooth, you see the flash of a trout. Will he take in June the fly your fingers are still making in January? Of course he will. He does, and you strike. It is the trembling of your fingers that brings you back to winter lamplight. This will never do. That hackle must be unwound and preened and wound again. But long before it is fairly wound and made fast the Vizier is again alone and the Caliph, you, is once more far away, this time six months younger and by another stream, catching, with a fly the very spit of this that is all but finished, the best trout you put in your basket last year.

It is waste of time, I say, to experiment in winter. Make, as well as you can, the flies that you can trust, partly because such flies have a past, of which they give you the freedom while you tie them, partly because you will otherwise never use them. A natural disposition to distrust new flies, together with a natural diffidence, will lead you, in summer, when the trout are rising, to try every fly you have in your box before risking the loss of a fish by offering some unorthodox, half-accidental mongrel tied by yourself. This, of course, applies particularly to flies for river fishing. Lake flies have a wider margin of permissible fantasy. But even for lake fishing, when I am tying them by lamplight, I prefer to make flies of the patterns I know I shall need. Some of them may, what with the Caliph's happy absences, be rough, but

> 'How poor a thing I sometimes find
> Will captivate a greedy mind.'

And if you run out of a standard pattern, Greenwell's Glory for example, losing your last in a good fish, you are happy to find even a poor specimen in a corner of your box. Poor as it may be, it has its family prestige. Even if it catch no fish in summer it has caught plenty in winter, while it was still in the vice. It has already the glamour of victory. You fish it with confidence and therefore well, and if it is your tail-fly you may at least get a trout on the dropper.

RICHARD JEFFERIES

THE HILLS AND THE VALE

With an introduction by Edward Thomas

This collection of Jefferies' essays, spanning the 1870s and 1880s, was brought together by Edward Thomas and published in 1909. Amongst them are examples from nearly every kind and period of Jefferies' work: he writes as reporter, archaeologist, sportsman, politician, naturalist, and philosopher. The book ends with some of the finest and most powerful of his nature writings, in which he grasps 'a meaning waiting in the grass and water' of a 'wider existence yet to be enjoyed on the earth'.

RICHARD JEFFERIES

THE GAMEKEEPER AT HOME and THE AMATEUR POACHER

With an introduction by Richard Fitter

With the first appearance of these two books in 1878 and 1879, Richard Jefferies was recognized as a nature writer of the first rank. *The Gamekeeper at Home* recaptures long hours of his early youth, and springs spontaneously from acute nostalgia for his native meadows and downs, woods and streams, aided by a razor-sharp memory for countryside sights and smells. *The Amateur Poacher* deals with the more illicit characters and pastimes of rural life: badger-baiting, ferreting, poaching the churchyard pheasants. It is perhaps the finest example of Jefferies' acute sensitivity to the moods of nature and his remarkable talent for articulating the essence of the countryside.